Written and researched by

Chris and Melanie Rice: updated by Andrew Costello

The contents of this guidebook are believed correct at the time of printing. Attractions and establishments may open, close or change and Thomas Cook Holdings Ltd cannot accept responsibility for errors or omissions, or for the consequences of any reliance on the information provided. Descriptions and assessments are based on the author's views and experience at the time of writing and these do not necessarily represent those of Thomas Cook Holdings. We would be grateful to be told of any changes or updates; please notify them to the Project Editor at the address below.

Thomas Cook Publishing, PO Box 227, Units 19–21 Coningsby Road, The Thomas Cook Business Park, Peterborough PE3 8XX, United Kingdom.
E-mail: books@thomascook.com

The Algarve: magical places

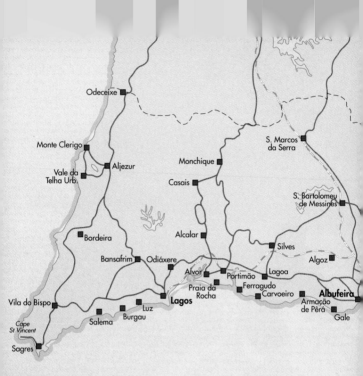

Odeceixe

Monte Clerigo

Vale da
Telha Urb.

Aljezur

Monchique

S. Marcos
da Serra

Casais

S. Bartolomeu
de Messines

Bordeira

Alcalar

Silves

Algoz

Bansafrim

Odiáxere

Alvor

Portimão

Lagoa

Praia da
Rocha

Ferragudo

Carvoeiro

Albufeira

Vila do Bispo

Lagos

Luz

Burgau

Armação
de Pêra

Salema

Gale

Cape
St Vincent

Sagres

ATLANTIC OCEAN

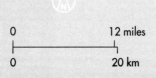

| 0 | 12 miles |
| 0 | 20 km |

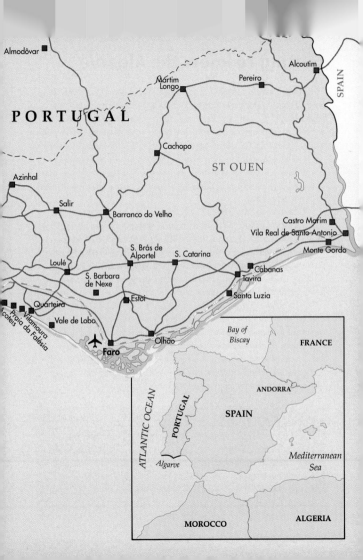

Getting to know the Algarve

More than 2 million European visitors head for the Algarve every year. Why do they come? For most people the climate is the main attraction – the Algarve basks in more than 3000 hours of sunshine per year; the winters are mild, the summers long and hot. Even in the coolest months temperatures rarely fall below 15°C, while in July and August 29°C is the norm. The beaches are another plus. In the eastern Algarve, the long, unbroken expanses of golden sand are ideal for swimming. In the west, a succession of bays, inlets and rocky coves, sheltered by distinctive sandstone cliffs, make magical places to laze the day away.

Those looking for a more active holiday will appreciate the first-class sporting facilities, including no fewer than 16 golf courses, designed to show off the beauties of the countryside as well as test the skills of the players. Besides golf there are opportunities for deep-sea fishing, windsurfing, horse riding, sailing, bowling, tennis, clay pigeon shooting, and even yoga and aerobics. Or, if all this sounds too exhausting, there are the dunes and cliff paths, perfect for a gentle ramble or an evening stroll.

The Algarve offers just as much variety in its nightlife. You can dine out at a romantic clifftop restaurant, on a terrace overlooking the beach or in a converted fisherman's cottage; stop for a sundowner in a cocktail bar on the promenade, or enjoy a pint of beer in an English-style pub. For a touch of local colour, sign up for a *fado* evening (see page 7) or village-restaurant barbecue. Then dance the night away in a disco or nightclub, or, if you are feeling lucky, have a flutter in one of the casinos.

AZULEJO TILES

Glazed, multi-coloured *azulejo* tiles began appearing in the Algarve more than 500 years ago and are now used to decorate everything from park benches to house fronts, restaurants and even railway stations. The oldest examples are in churches and chapels, where the predominantly blue tiles usually depict biblical scenes.

WHAT IS *FADO*?

Fado music is as important to the Portuguese as *flamenco* is to the Spanish. *Fado* ballads are plaintive and dramatic, usually about lost or unrequited love and the vicissitudes of life. The singer, or *fadista,* traditionally wears black to commemorate Maria Severa, a famous 19th-century performer who died tragically young. The accompaniment is provided by two guitarists.

THE PORTUGUESE EXPERIENCE

Algarvians are a welcoming and hospitable people (characteristics they are said to have inherited from the Moors). Go along to a *baile,* a riotous village knees-up usually involving the entire community. The energetic dancing is accompanied by accordions, fiddles, triangles and side drums, sometimes even bagpipes. You will find the uninhibited Algarvian sense of fun and enjoyment infectious.

Praia d'Alvor

The best of the Algarve

CASTLES AND FORTRESSES

- **Silves** (*page 75*) was the ancient capital of the Algarve and the last stronghold of the Moors; the red sandstone castle was partly restored during the Second World War.
- The harbour fortress at **Lagos** (*page 63*) has been restored and is now a small museum.
- At **Loulé** (*page 79*) and **Castro Marim,** near Monte Gordo, (*see map page 5*) the remains of the medieval battlements have survived offering superb views of the surrounding countryside.

EATING AND DRINKING

- Take a picnic to the 'end of the world' at **Cape St Vincent**, near Sagres (*page 59*).
- Sample chicken *piri-piri* at the 'top of the world' otherwise known as **Fóia** (*page 67*), the highest point in the Serra de Monchique.
- Dine close to the Spanish border at **Alcoutim** and enjoy a splendid view across the River Guadiana.
- Sip a cocktail on a terrace at **Praia da Rocha** (*page 22*) and watch the rays of the setting sun light up the sandstone cliffs.
- Take a **boat trip** (*page 43*) along the coast and share a barbecue lunch on board with fellow passengers.
- Enjoy fresh sardines in a riverside restaurant in **Portimão** (*page 71*).
- Dine in the sophisticated surroundings of **Vilamoura marina** (*page 42*), where the lights from the boats, bars and restaurants shimmer in the water.

BEST BEACHES

- The Algarve has more than 60 named beaches, all washed clean by Atlantic tides.
- There are several contenders for the title of longest beach: **Falesia**, near Albufeira (*page 35*), **Armação de Pêra** (*page 27*), **Quarteira-Vilamoura** (*pages 42–49*) and **Monte Gordo** (*page 55*) are the strongest candidates.

- The prize for the widest swathe of sand (100m, over 300ft) must go to **Praia da Rocha** (*page 22*).

- **Praia de Faro** (*page 83*), **Meia Praia** (near Alvor, *page 18*) and **Martinhal** (near Sagres, *page 60*) are good windsurfing beaches.

- **Burgau** (*page 10*) and **Baleeira** (near Albufeira, *page 35*) have excellent conditions for snorkelling and scuba diving.

ACTIVITIES

- Take a canoe ride on the scenic **Arade River**.

- Enjoy the variety of challenges offered by the Algarve's **16 golf courses** (*pages 32, 43 and 52*).

- Join a **boat excursion** exploring the grottoes, tunnels and unusual rock formations typical of the western Algarve (*page 108*).

- Go **scuba diving** in the clear waters off Ponta da Piedade near Lagos (*page 111*).

- Try your hand at **big-game fishing** (*page 111*). Boats leave from Portimão, Vilamoura and Sagres.

- Learn to **windsurf** at Praia da Rocha (*page 22*), or take on the bigger waves on the west coast.

- Joining a **horse-riding expedition** is one of the best ways of becoming acquainted with the beauty of the Algarvian countryside; alternatively hire a **mountain bike** (*page 111*).

EXCURSIONS

- Visit **Lisbon**, the Portuguese capital and see a different face of Portugal (*page 91*).

- Go on a **jeep safari** in the Monchique Mountains (*page 67*).

- Cross the border into Spain at **Vila Real de Santo António** (*page 55*), or visit the beautiful historic city of **Sevilla** (*page 95*).

- Take a bus to **Loulé** on a Saturday when it is home to the largest gypsy market in the Algarve (*page 80*).

- Explore the **Ria Formosa nature reserve** or the wild beaches of the west coast (*page 87*).

Salema's beach

Salema and Burgau –
small is beautiful

Typical red-roofed fishermen's houses, a small sandy
beach and cobbled streets rising gently up sandstone
cliffs, characterise both the villages of Salema
(pronounced 'Sah-*lay*-mah') and Burgau (pronounced
'*Bur*-gow'). With just a handful of shops, bars and
restaurants, holidaymakers come here to enjoy the
peace and quiet as well as the stunning scenery of
the western Algarve.

Life in these tiny communities revolves around the harbour where the local fishermen mend their nets and wash out the squid pots. Boat trips head along the coast from Salema harbour to the rocky crevices of Ponta da Piedade where egrets nest or, in the opposite direction, where swimmers can enjoy a dip before sitting down to a barbecue on a secluded beach. The beauty of the area can also be appreciated on foot by following the two-hour switchback walk over the headlands between Burgau and Salema, which takes in the remote coves of Ponta da Almadena and Boca do Rio.

 Wake up in time to watch the sun rising over the bay and you will see the fishermen hauling in the first catch of the day; alternatively, you can enjoy their harvest at lunchtime by sampling grilled sardines in a harbour restaurant.

THINGS TO SEE AND DO

Birdwatching
Full- and half-day trips, led by an expert ornithologist, can be booked through the tourist offices at Portimão (*tel: 282 416556*) and Lagos (*tel: 282 763031*).

Burgau Sports Centre
The facilities here include a gym, football, basketball, tennis and squash courts, swimming pool and aerobics sessions, plus a children's playground and children's sports mornings. *Burgau. Tel: 282 697350.*

SHOPPING
- There is a newsagent, a supermarket and a souvenir shop on Rua 25 de Abril in Burgau.
- Salema has a couple of supermarkets as well as handicraft and souvenir shops on the waterfront. At Loja do Tosca you will find top quality one-off designer Portuguese and ethnic clothing and accessories (beautiful belts and shoes). Splendid sculptures also for sale. *Rua dos Pescadores, Salema. Open daily 0900–late.*
- The nearest banks and pharmacies are in Praia da Luz. For more comprehensive shopping, head for Lagos.

Parque da Floresta Golf and Leisure Resort

The excellent Parque da Floresta club offers lawn bowling (1000–dusk, competitions Mon), an 18-hole golf course plus golf academy, four tennis courts, a fitness and leisure centre, mountain bike hire, archery (with very cheap 'have-a-go sessions' Sat–Wed 1300–1700) and walking tours. *Vale do Poço, Budens. Tel: 282 690000.*

RESTAURANTS AND BARS

Salema:

 Atabua Cocktail Bar ££ The place to be seen in Salema with a cocktail, *sangria*, English, German or Portuguese beer in hand. *Rua dos Pescadores. Open daily 2030–0200.*

 Atlantica ££ A beach restaurant with an extensive fish menu, including clams, tuna and *cataplana* (fish stew). *Praia da Salema. Tel: 282 65142. Open daily 1000–late.*

 Boia Restaurant Bar ££ Sip cocktails, enjoy fresh fish, and take in the sea views. *Rua dos Pescadores. Open 1000–0200.*

 **O Carapau Francês £–££** Attractive, informal pizza restaurant-café which also does fish and meat dishes. Eat on the pretty terrace or in the traditional tiled interior. *Main Square. Tel: 282 695253. Open daily 0900–late.*

 Mira Mar ££ Good food is available all day at reasonable prices in this typical Algarvian restaurant. The grilled swordfish is recommended. *Praia da Salema. Tel: 282 657250. Open 0900–late.*

Restaurant Florestal ££–£££ Set among pines and eucalyptus trees, this friendly place offers an international menu, with real home-made American-style burgers at lunchtime. *Barão de São João. Tel: 282 687204. Open Mar–Oct: lunch 1200–1400, snacks 1400–1900, dinner 1900–2200. Closed Nov–Apr and every Tues.*

Burgau:

 Ancora ££–£££ Smart Portuguese eatery. Vegetarian meals are available with 24 hours' notice. *Largo dos Pescadores. Tel: 282 697102. Open 1900–2300. Closed Mon–Tues.*

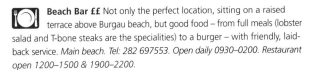 **Beach Bar ££** Not only the perfect location, sitting on a raised terrace above Burgau beach, but good food – from full meals (lobster salad and T-bone steaks are the specialities) to a burger – with friendly, laid-back service. *Main beach. Tel: 282 697553. Open daily 0930–0200. Restaurant open 1200–1500 & 1900–2200.*

Caravela ££–£££ Portuguese cuisine is served under palm trees in the garden of this charming restaurant. Try the saddle of lamb, stewed rabbit hunter style or turbot in breadcrumbs. *Rua Valedo. Tel: 282 69274. Open 1830–2230.*

Casa Grande £££ *One Foot in the Algarve* was filmed in this charming old manor house and its former winery is now a restaurant serving up a varied Portuguese menu with a good choice for vegetarians. Occasional live music. *Road to Praia da Luz. Tel: 282 697416. Open Mar–Nov Mon–Fri 1900–midnight. Closed weekends and Dec–Feb.*

Dom Dinis ££ Set in a very peaceful location, Dom Dinis is a long-established traditional rustic international/Portuguese restaurant. *1km from Burgau on the Salema road. Tel: 282 697461. Open 1000–1500 & 1830–2230 (bar until 0200).*

Rios Negros ££ Fish (caught daily by the owner-chef) and meat dishes grilled on an open fire are served up in this popular, cosy restaurant. Jazz and popular music. *Largo do Poço 4 (N125 between Burgau and Budens). Tel: 282 695330. Open 1930–2300.*

The sheltered waters of Luz

Praia da Luz – rock slabs and sand

Whitewashed villas and holiday apartments cloaked in bougainvillaea blend harmoniously with the picturesque old houses that cluster round the fishing harbour of Luz (pronounced 'Loosh'). The beach of soft sand is edged by great slabs of flat smooth rocks, which make perfect sunbathing beds for visitors who prefer not to get sand between their toes. The sheltered waters of the bay are ideal for water-skiing, windsurfing, sailing and diving. Luz has its own local shops, a sprinkling of bars and restaurants and even a discotheque near the waterfront.

Luz's attractive hinterland is ideal for walks and drives. A short stroll up the path from the car park at the eastern end of the village will take you to the top of the headland, where an *atalaia* (obelisk) stands at a height of 108m (360ft) above sea level. From here there are coastal views as far as Sagres.

The gently rolling hills to the north of Luz can best be explored by car. The road winds through a landscape dotted with farms, ancient wells, fig trees, and quaint villages like Barão de São João.

THINGS TO SEE AND DO

Fortaleza *
Luz's fortress was built in the 16th century and has been beautifully restored to house a fine restaurant (*see page 17*). Even if you don't intend eating here, don't be shy to ask to look in.

Horse riding
Tiffany's Riding Centre caters for young and old, novices and experts alike, and offers rides lasting from one hour to a whole holiday course. *Vale Grifo, Almádena. Tel: 282 697395. Open daily.*

Parish church *
Picturesquely situated near the waterfront of the old village is the parish church, with medieval vaults and a gilded baroque altar.

Sea Sports Centre
This licensed diving school hires out equipment and offers lessons for beginners and advanced divers. *Avenida dos Pescadores, Loja 4. Tel: 282 789538.*

Sports
Facilities at the Luz Bay and Ocean Clubs include swimming pools, saunas, a Turkish bath, gym, mini-golf, tennis and squash courts.

Watersports School
Windsurfing, sailing and water-skiing are all available. *Praia da Luz. Tel: 282 778581.*

SHOPPING

The Centro Commercial on the seafront has a number of useful outlets selling clothes, food, magazines and groceries. There is a large **Alisuper** supermarket near the church. Situated below the Dolphin restaurant (*see below*), the colourful **Africa Craft Shop** specialises in curios and handicrafts from southern Africa. *Rua da Calheta. Open 1400–2100.*

RESTAURANTS

Bar Carib ££ A restaurant with a swimming pool and tennis court (racket and balls for hire) – great for family lunches. The special barbecue (Sun lunchtime and Wed evening) is a bargain. Sandwiches and children's meals also available. *Montinhos da Luz, 1km from Praia da Luz. Tel: 282 788908. Open 1000–late.*

Cangalho ££–£££ Portuguese cuisine served in a traditional farmhouse setting. Home-baked bread, roast pig and chicken *cabidela* (stewed in a rich sauce with rice) are among the specialities here. *Quinta Figueiras, Sítio do Medronho, Barão de São João. Tel: 282 697218. Open 1200–1500 & 1800–2200. Closed Mon.*

Dolphin ££–£££ Restaurant with sea views from the patio, serving Portuguese and international cuisine, plus some interesting South African specials. *Rua da Calheta 14A. Tel: 282 789992. Open 1830–2200 (last meal). Closed Dec–Jan.*

Duke of Holland £–££ English-run bar and restaurant offering all kinds of food from snacks to full meals. Steaks in sauces are their speciality. Quiz and karaoke nights. *Rua da Praia 19. Tel: 282 789888. Open daily 1900–0200.*

Esplanada da Fortaleza ££ Modern international cooking, including inventive pizzas, lots of vegetarian choices, and great cakes during the day, make up the menu at this excellent new airy informal terrace restaurant which shares the same grounds as the historic Fortaleza. Wonderful views to the rocky beach below. *Open daily 1000–2200.*

Fontenário ££ Family-orientated restaurant, serving international and local dishes. There are vegetarian choices and a reasonably priced tourist menu. *Espiche. Tel: 282 789953. Open 1000–2300 (from 1900 in winter).*

Fortaleza da Luz £££ Housed in a beautifully restored, very atmospheric 16th-century fort, this Portuguese restaurant, with fantastic views of the coast, is perfect for that special romantic occasion. *Rua da Igreja 3. Tel: 282 789926. Open 1230–1500 & 1900–2200 (last meal order).*

Godots ££–£££ English-run restaurant offering grilled meat and fish as well as vegetarian dishes on a predominantly international menu. Outside terrace. Relaxed atmosphere. *Rua 25 de Abril. Tel: 282 789647. Open 1900–2200 (last meal order). Closed Sun & Wed.*

Luz Tavern £–££ Full English breakfast and a choice of British beers for the homesick with Portuguese and international dishes for the more adventurous. Pub games, Satellite TV, quiz nights (Mon and Fri). *Largo da República. Tel: 282 789179. Open daily 0900–0200.*

Maharaja da Luz ££ Good northern Indian food with a take-away service. *Centro Comercial, Edificio Luz Tur (above the pharmacy). Tel: 282 789579. Open 1200–1430 & 1800–midnight.*

NIGHTLIFE

The Bull Small, cosy pub with an upstairs restaurant featuring fine views of the rocky beach. *Rua da Calheta 5.*

Mirage Popular disco-cocktail bar, with a restaurant serving an interesting and varied menu. Happy hour 2200–2300. *Ocean Club complex. Bar open daily 1900–0200. Restaurant open 1900–2230. Closed Sun.*

Le Privé Club serving up Portuguese and English pop music. *Rua José da Conceição Conde, beneath Centro Commercial Via Sul. Open 2300–0400.*

Alvor's icing-sugar parish church

Alvor – picture-postcard resort

Perfect for a relaxing holiday, Alvor is a picture-postcard resort, handy for the nightclubs of Praia da Rocha on the one hand and the historic sights of Lagos on the other.

The focal point of the Alvor is Torralta beach, a kilometre-long stretch of fine golden sand with sun-loungers, umbrellas and pedalos for hire. A 15-minute stroll over the hill brings you to the old village. Here the fishermen bring their catches to market at dawn while villagers can be seen wading into the estuary – the habitat of stilts, terns and other wetland birds – to collect shellfish for the local restaurants. On the other side of the harbour is the 16th-century parish church with typical Manueline stone carvings.

THINGS TO SEE AND DO

Ethnographical Museum *
Tiny old-fashioned museum next to the small church of Santa Casa de Misericórdia, tracing Alvor's fishing roots. *Rua Marquês de Pombal. Open daily. Small admission fee.*

Folk dancing
The Hotel Delfim holds alternate evenings of folk dancing and traditional *fado* music on Tuesdays. *Hotel Delfim, Praia dos Três Irmãos. Tel: 282 458901.*

Golf
Laid out on sandstone cliffs with superb views of the Serra de Monchique, Alto Golf is a taxing 73-par course, designed by Sir Henry Cotton and famous for its 604m (2000ft) 16th hole, one of the longest in Europe. As well as the main course, there is a golf school with practice bunker. *Tel: 282 420200.*

Horse riding and jeep safaris
Vale de Ferro Riding offers scenic, cross-country excursions through the hinterland of Portimão. Beginners and experienced riders are all welcome. Jeep safaris can also be arranged into the mountains at Monchique. *Ask your holiday representative for further details.*

Lawn bowling and tennis
The San António Lawn Bowling and Country Club has tennis and squash courts, swimming pools, sauna, a Turkish bath, aerobic classes and a beauty salon among its facilities. There are special-offer prices to include two to three hours' bowling and lunch. *Montes de Alvor. Tel: 282 495713. Restaurant and bar open daily 1000–2200 (0930–1900 in winter).*

Ten-pin bowling
Torralta Bowling has four bowling lanes, snooker, pool, pinball machines and bar. *Praia de Alvor. Tel: 282 458663. Open daily 1400–0200.*

Wetlands
The estuaries of the Alvor and the Odiáxere are rich in birdlife, and (for the time being at least) protected from developers. Explore the salt pans via the raised footpath.

RESTAURANTS AND BARS

Ababuja ££ Set in a traditional house with a wooden front porch this atmospheric fish restaurant occupies a prime site overlooking the harbour. *Rua da Ribeira. Tel: 282 458979. Open 1200–2230/2300.*

Albar £–££ Despite its snack-bar appearance, the Albar serves very good Portuguese and international full meals. The atmosphere is lively but not hectic, service is friendly and fast and it's a perfect place for people-watching. *Rua Marquês de Pombal 21. Tel: 282 457124. Open daily 1000–late.*

Alvila ££–£££ This long-established restaurant is renowned for its Portuguese-international food and the quality of the *fado* every Tues. *Amoreira-Alvor (near Hotel Delfim). Tel: 282 458775. Open Thur–Tues 1230–1430 & 1900–2230. Closed Wed.*

L'Angolo Ristorante Italiano £–££ Charming small pizza-pasta house by the church. Friendly staff, nice atmosphere. *Rua 28 de Septembro. Tel: 282 458369. Open 1100–1500 & 1800–late, Wed–Mon. Closed Tues.*

Borala £–££ Live music nightly from 2200 in this trendy bar. *Rua Dr Fredrico Ramos Mendes 17.*

China Garden ££ The food here is excellent quality, beautifully presented and very good value. Friendly staff and a nice relaxed dining room. *Rua Dr Alfonso Costa 43. Tel: 282 457284. Open daily 1200–1500 & 1800–late.*

Grande Muralha £–££ Run by the same team as the China Garden (*see above*) to the same high standards, this is ideal for a quick Chinese meal or a takeaway. The service is fast and the value is unbeatable. *Rua D João II (bottom of hill). Tel: 282 457154. Open 1200–1500 & 1800–2330.*

Hellman's ££ Hellman's offers modern, imaginative Portuguese and international cuisine in a lovely traditional house with lively young staff. Book the top floor for great views. *Travessa da Ribeira. Tel: 282 458208. Open daily 1800–2230.*

Mourisco Bar £ The beautiful Moorish interior of this bar has brought a little bit of the Alhambra to Alvor. Cheap beer, very good service, lively and noisy by night. *Rua Dr Frederico Ramos Mendes.*

 Os Marafados ££ Formerly known as the Green Room, this lively and popular restaurant-bar serves international food and is always packed. *Rua Dr Frederico Ramos Mendes. Tel: 282 457265. Open 1000–late.*

 Paddy's Bar £–££ Irish-style bar with a rooftop terrace. *Rua Dr António José de Almeida 9.*

 Somewhere Else £–£££ Cook your own fish or meat on a stone grill in this cosmopolitan, friendly Irish Dutch-run Portuguese restaurant. *Rua Poeta João de Deus. Tel: 282 458595. Open 1200–2300.*

 Tasca do Guedès ££ It's not on the main drag so Snr Guedès and family try that bit harder. Lovely rustic nautical-themed *típica* restaurant serving superb fish and shellfish dishes. Try the *cataplana* (see page 99). *Rua dos Pescadores 25. Tel: 282 458528. Open daily 1200–1500 & 1900–2200.*

 Tasca Morais £–££ The real thing! Charming, old-fashioned traditional Alvor house serving good local food to locals and visitors. Very friendly service. *Rua Dr António José de Almeida 14. Tel: 282 459392. Open Thur–Tues 1830–2230. Closed Wed.*

 Vagabundo ££–£££ The nicest dining room in town, the Vagabundo is set in a traditional house on the main street with a large open aspect and a lovely rear garden. Excellent inventive Portuguese/international menu (try the Madeira kebab). *Rua Dr Frederico Ramos Mendes. Tel: 282 458726. Open daily 1800–2230.*

FISH RESTAURANTS

If you like barbecued fresh fish, it's hard to go wrong in Alvor. The restaurants at the foot of the hill fronting on to the harbour are all good. **Tony and Ria's (££)** is a favourite; if you're on a budget go to **Tasca Morgandinho (£)**.

The 'beach of the rocks'

Praia da Rocha – fun resort

Praia da Rocha (pronounced 'Pryah da Rosha') is
shamelessly brash, a fun resort with generous helpings
of sun, sea and sand. The name means 'beach of the
rocks', an allusion to the spectacular outcrops of red
and yellow sandstone which feature on so many
postcards. There's more than enough room for
sunbathers on the 100m-wide swathe of sand, but
just to make sure, a tunnel carved through the west
cliff opens up the more secluded bays beyond.

SHOPPING

There are two supermarkets, **Alisuper** and **Himalaia**, on Avenida Tomás Cabreira. There is a 'gypsy market' on the road to Portimão (close to Clube Praia da Rocha) on the first Monday of each month.

THINGS TO SEE AND DO

Rocha Express

The tourist train leaves the Miradouro at half-hourly intervals (1000–1200 & 1600–2330), calling at Fortaleza and Praia do Vau. *Tickets can be bought on board.*

Ten-pin bowling

Praia da Rocha bowling alley has four lanes, plus video games, pool, table football and a bar. *Avenida Tomás Cabreira. Open daily 1000–0200.*

Watersports

Water-skiing and pedalo hire (including snorkels) are all available from the beach. Praia da Rocha also has excellent conditions for windsurfing – boards can be rented by the hour with lessons for beginners.

RESTAURANTS

Almeida ££ Civilised place to eat with a classy tiled interior and pale pink tablecloths, serving Portuguese/international food. *Avenida Tomás Cabreira. Tel: 282 427075. Open daily 1200–late.*

Cabassa ££ Set on a lawn on the quiet eastern part of the seafront, this is a delightful terrace restaurant known for its high-quality inventive Italian cooking and excellent 'barbecue nights'. Speedy, friendly service. *Avenida Tomás Cabreira. Tel: 282 424307. Open daily 1800–late.*

A Casa de Rocha ££–£££ Highly rated restaurant set in one of the resort's original 1930s summer villas, serving top-quality shellfish and Portuguese specials. *Sitio dos Castelos, Avenida Tomás Cabreira. Tel: 282 419674. Open Tues–Sun (closed Sun lunch) 1200– 1500 & 1800–2200.*

Casalinho ££ Right on the beach, Casalinho may not look much but it has a loyal army of fans who come here for top-quality Portuguese/international cooking with flambé specials. *Main beach, down steps by Penguin. Tel: 282 422579. Open 0930–2230.*

Chez Benny ££ Noted for some of the best salads in the area, Chez Benny also serves good pizzas and crêpes. The pretty restaurant overlooks the beach and is festooned with numerous flowers and plants. *Avenida Tomás Cabreira. Tel: 282 483224. Open daily 1200–late.*

Churrasqueira £ Cheap and cheerful first-floor café with excellent views of the beach and coast: chicken *piri-piri* is the speciality. *Avenida Tomás Cabreira.*

Fagin's £ Take-away fish and chip shop with fish fingers for children and mouthwatering spit-roasted chicken. *Edifício Rochamar. Open 0900–midnight.*

Falésia ££ Set in an old house with modern new extensions and boasting a superb clifftop position, the Falésia is one of Praia da Rocha's favourite eating houses. Extensive international menu. *Avenida Tomás Cabreira. Tel: 282 423524.*

Nova China £–££ reasonably priced Chinese, with an excellent take-away service. *Edifício San José, Avenida Tomás Cabreira. Tel: 282 415404. Open daily 1200–1500 & 1800–late.*

Olivers £ Authentic English food from breakfasts to bangers 'n' mash and Sunday roast. *Edifício Rochamar. Tel: 282 411862. Open 0900–0200.*

Panorâmico ££ Smart friendly restaurant serving an excellent selection of quality meals. *Next to Katedral disco. Tel: 282 417268. Open 1200–late.*

 Safari ££ Under the same management for over 22 years, Safari mixes a mostly international menu with special dishes from Angola. Nice old house, lovely terrace. *Avenida Tomás Cabreira. Tel: 282 423540. Open daily 1200–2230/2300.*

 O Terraço de Penguin ££ Long established and with a magnificently sited terrace, the Penguin is the nicest place to eat in Praia da Rocha. Excellent service and an adventurous menu (everything is home-made) with good choices for vegetarians. *Avenida Tomás Cabreira. Tel: 282 483623. Open daily 1200–midnight.*

 Titanic £££ Dress up for a special evening out at this relaxing flambé and fish restaurant, with a wide choice of international dishes. *Rua Eng Francisco Bivar. Tel: 282 422371.*

NIGHTLIFE

Babylone Lively disco club with a large dance floor. *Edifício Tropical Rocha. Open 2300–0600.*

Casino American roulette, French roulette, Black Jack, Punto e Banca and 306 slot machines will relieve you of your *euros* here. Dinner is served at 2030 nightly followed by a Las Vegas-style show at 2230. *Hotel Algarve, Avenida Tomás Cabreira. Tel: 282 415001. Open daily 1600–0400. Passport required.*

Colombus Disco bar known for its cocktails. *Edifício Rio a Vista. Open 1200–0400.*

Katedral Large nightclub with bars, Satellite TV, pool tables and disco. *Avenida Tomás Cabreira. Open 2300–0730.*

On the Rocks Praia da Rocha's trendiest cocktail bar and disco with terrace overlooking the beach. Happy hour 1000–2030. *Avenida Tomás Cabreira. Open 1000–0400.*

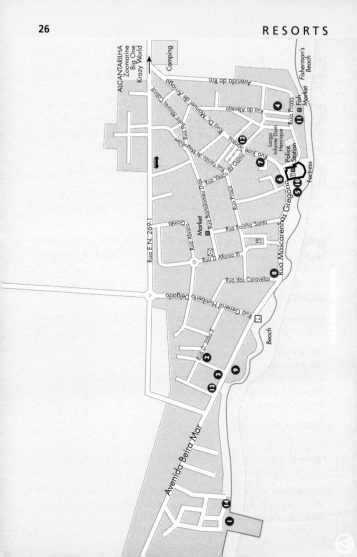

Armação de Pêra –
the Algarve's longest beach

Palm trees shade the promenade at Armação de Pêra (pronounced 'Arma*sau* de Perra'), a modern resort boasting one of the longest expanses of sand in the Algarve. In fact, it stretches all the way to Galé, a satellite of Albufeira.

To the east of the resort is Fisherman's Beach, where, early in the morning, colourful small boats depart as they have done for centuries, in search of the catch of the day. Get here at about 1000 to see them return with their booty. The old part of Armação de Pêra lies in the cobbled streets behind the beach and here you'll find the local bars and fish restaurants. To the west of the resort are the Algarve's classic picture-postcard rock stacks and cliffs. Boat trips from the beach pass these on their way to the spectacular stacks and caves between here and Carvoeiro (*page 30*).

THINGS TO SEE AND DO

Walk to Senhora da Rocha
'Our Lady of the Rock' is a sailor's chapel, dating from the 16th century, perched on a spectacular headland around 3km west of the resort. If you make the effort to climb up to the chapel, the interior contains some lovely *azulejos* (tiles) and votive model-ship offerings (check on opening times first with the Turismo in Armação de Pêra). A rock-cut tunnel gives access to the lovely beach of Senhora da Rocha.

Visit Alcantarilha
Alcantarilha has a notorious traffic bottleneck on the N125. Get off the main road here and go to the landmark church, which has a macabre chapel lined with human skulls and bones. There is nothing sinister about this. They are simply the remains of some 1500 parishioners, permanently exhibited as a cheerful reminder of human mortality!

Golf

Created only in 1994, Salgados is a links-style 18-hole course of 6080m (over 6750 yards), chock-a-block with water hazards; high handicap players should make sure they have plenty of balls in reserve! Handicap certificate required. *Vale de Parra. Tel: 289 591111.*

SHOPPING

Porches is famous for its pottery. Watch the potters at work before purchasing genuine hand-painted ceramics from any of the outlets, which are located along the main N125 highway.

RESTAURANTS *(see map on page 26)*

 Casa d'Italia ££ ❶ Imagine yourself as the guest in a private country villa as you enjoy authentic Italian food at shaded tables set around a pool, with hillside and sea views. Quality at surprisingly modest prices. *Ald Porches Praia, Sra da Rocha (signposted opposite Hotel Viking). Tel: 282 310847. Open 1030–midnight. Meals 1230–1500 & 1900–2230.*

 O Fernando ££ ❷ Excellent fish dishes are served in this typical Portuguese restaurant. Try the grilled fresh salmon. *Rua Rosa dos Ventos. Tel: 282 313481. Open 1000–midnight.*

 Gelataria Penguin £ ❸ A promenade café selling ice-creams, crêpes, sandwiches and other snacks. *Avenida Beira Mar.*

 A Grelha ££ ❹ It's claimed to be 'the oldest traditional restaurant' in the Algarve – it's certainly one of its best for fresh fish and seafood, though it also offers a good selection of meat dishes. *Rua do Alentejo 2. Tel: 282 312245. Open daily 1200–1500 & 1800–2200/2230.*

 Jony Beach Bar ££ ❺ A great setting, right on the beachfront, for inexpensive fresh fish and seafood, or just a drink and a snack. *Beachfront, by Fortaleza. Tel: 282 342201. Open 1000–2300.*

 Kam Kong ££ ❻ Excellent Chinese food. Specialities include crispy duck with pancakes. *Largo 25 de Abril. Tel: 282 312196. Open 1800–midnight.*

Pizzaria Gabi £ ❼ Cheap and cheerful pizzeria for when you want a simple but satisfying snack. *Rua José António Santos. Tel: 282 312883. Open 1200–late.*

 Porters ££ ❽ Warm and friendly service guaranteed at this traditional Portuguese restaurant specialising in *cataplana* (fish stew, see page 99), but also serving such favourites as lasagne, prawn kebabs, savoury pancakes and steak. *Rua das Caravelas. Tel: 282 313434. Open daily 1200–1500 & 1700–late.*

 Raj ££ ❾ Excellent value-for-money Indian cuisine, and a wonderful setting – with great views from the patio overlooking the sea. *Hotel Garbe. Tel: 282 315187, ext 63. Open daily 1230–1430 & 1830–2330.*

Fresh fish – from sea to boat to restaurant

 Rocha da Palha ££ ❿ When other places are empty the locals pack out this simple fish grill bar overlooking the beach. They must know something! *Beachfront, Largo da Fortaleza. Tel: 96 516615. Open daily 1200–1500 & 1800–2200.*

 Serol ££ ⓫ At the entrance to the fisherman's quarter, Serol is highly recommended for its fish, shellfish and various *cataplanas* (indoor dining only). *Rua Portas do Mar 2. Tel: 282 312146. Open Thur–Tues 1200–1530 & 1900–2230. Closed Wed.*

NIGHTLIFE

Havanna ⓬ Trendy cocktail bar with resident parrot. *Rua Dr Martinho Simoes. Open daily 1900–late.*

The Runner ⓭ Friendly, English-style pub with satellite TV, bar meals and snacks served all day. *Avenida Beira Mar. Open daily 1100–late.*

Sebastian's ⓮ Located in the Hotel Viking, the only nightclub in Armação da Pêra takes an underworld theme for its décor. *Hotel Viking, Senhora da Rocha. Open Fri–Sat 2130–late.*

Carvoeiro's sheltered cove

Carvoeiro –
sandy coves and sea caves

Armação de Pêra's smaller neighbour, Carvoeiro
(pronounced 'Carvo*whe*roh'), is highly photogenic
with brightly painted fishing boats and spruce,
whitewashed villas. Reached by a long and narrow
valley road, which eventually ends in a pocket-
handkerchief of golden sand, Carvoeiro is one of
the prettiest resorts in the Algarve.

THINGS TO SEE AND DO

Horse riding
'Casa Galaraz' stable, located near the beach at Carvoeiro, has a special park for children. Experienced staff offer guided horse rides and instruction. *Estrada de Benagil. Tel: 282 358055.*

Slide and Splash
Whirlpools and waterslides, including the new 'Black Hole', are among the features of this popular fun park. Facilities include shops, bars and a restaurant. Slide and Splash runs buses with pick-up points all along the coast (ask your holiday representative for further details). *N125, Vale de Deus, Estombar. Tel: 282 341685. Open daily 1000–1800. Admission charge.*

Tennis
Rocha Brava Tennis Club Improve your game or learn to play in a lovely location. *Rocha Brava. Tel: 282 357847.*

Wine tasting
Lagoa is famous for rough red wines with a high alcohol content. The Lagoa Wine Co-operative, on the Portimão road, opens its cellars for conducted tours and wine tastings. *Usually open 0930–1230 & 1400–1730, but tel: 282 342181 to check. It is advisable to book at least 24 hours in advance.*

SHOPPING
On Rua dos Pescadores, **A Praça Velha**, the outdoor 'Old Market' (*open daily*), deals mostly in mass-produced pottery though there are other handicrafts and souvenirs for sale. For better quality pottery go to **Porches** (*see Armação de Pêra, page 28*). The nearest real market to Carvoeiro is at **Lagoa** on the second Sunday of each month. Also on the main N125 road at Lagoa is **Mundo do Sapato** (Shoe World), not as big as it sounds (or looks from the road), but with some bargain brand-name footwear to be snapped up.

GOLF

● **Vale de Milho:** Designed by Ryder Cup player, Dave Thomas, architect of the Belfry Brabazon Course, this attractive course is surprisingly challenging for every golfer. Water hazards play a part in four of the nine holes on the par 30 course. Ideal for practising your short game and excellent value for money. *Tel: 282 358502.*

● **Pinta Pestana Golf Resort:** a new, well-designed 18-hole course, built around an ancient olive grove. Although it is a championship-class course, it is suitable for all handicap levels.

● The renowned *David Leadbetter Golf Academy* is also based here along with practice areas, shop, restaurant and bar. *Tel: 282 340900.*

BEACHES

Rocky promontories and crumbling sandstone cliffs, concealing a succession of inviting coves and grottoes, characterise this typical stretch of Algarvian coastline. The gently shelving beach at **Vale de Centianes** (approached by a flight of steps) is excellent for surfing. At **Algar Seco** the cliff forms a double arch, bridging the entrance to a cavernous lagoon of deep, clear water – a snorkeller's paradise. A small road train, the *Jumbolino*, travels the 4km (2.5 miles) east to **Praia do Carvalho** (also known as 'Smugglers Cove') but two other beaches well worth going that extra mile or so for are the coves of **Praia de Benagil** and **Praia da Marinha**.

RESTAURANTS

O Cantinho ££ Smart but informal family-run restaurant with an attractive terrace in a classy navy-and-white striped colour scheme. Portuguese/international cooking with specials, including chicken in the pot, *tournedos* of the house and *cataplana*. Estrada do Farol. *Tel: 282 358234. Open Tues–Sun 1200–1500 & 1800–2300. Closed Mon.*

O Chefe António ££ The shocking-pink colour scheme is simply a reflection of the flamboyant nature of the eponymous owner-chef, António! His chicken curry, leg of lamb, flambé dishes and meat kebabs are local legends. *Estrada do Farol. Tel: 282 358937. Open daily 1800–2230/2300.*

 Grande Muralha ££ The best Chinese restaurant in the area, offering all the usual favourites. *Estrada do Farol. Tel: 282 357380. Open daily 1200–1500 & 1800–2330.*

 Happy's ££ This cheerful Dutch-run restaurant serves international and Portuguese specialities in a cosy atmosphere. *Estrada do Farol. Tel: 282 357692. Open Mon–Sat 1200–2300. Closed Sun.*

 Stone Steak ££–£££ Cook your steak, fish or prawns the healthy and tasty way on sizzling stone grills. *Monte Carvoeiro. Tel: 282 357730. Open daily 1800–2300.*

NIGHTLIFE

Bote Carvoeiro's only disco, set right on the beachfront, with foam parties held every Wednesday. *Praia da Carvoeiro. Open 2300–0600.*

Jailhouse Set in a converted wine cellar, the long-established Jailhouse features nightly live music and disco favourites going back to the 1960s. It also has a beer garden. *Rua do Escondidinho 9. Open 1800–late. Music 2230.*

Manoel's Jazz Club Manoel and his sax have attained folk-hero status, creating this excellent jazz club. *Monte Carvoeiro. Open nightly 2230–late.*

Mungos Atmospheric British-style pub featuring live bands three or four times a week, plus quiz nights, Sky TV, dance competitions, bingo and a nightly disco. *Cerro dos Pios 17, Estrada do Farol. Tel: 282 356621. Open daily 0900–late.*

Round-up Saloon Great for country and western fans and anyone looking for a chance to find out what line dancing (Mon) is all about. Change your money into dollars at the Wild West bank (complete with a prison for miscreants) and enjoy, snacks, inexpensive drinks, karaoke and live piano music. *Estrada do Farol. Tel: 282 357009. Open daily 1800–0200.*

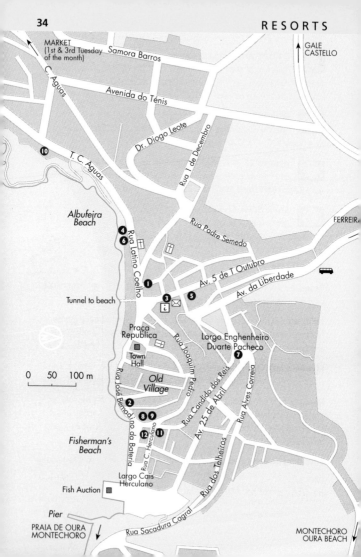

MARKET
(1st & 3rd Tuesday
of the month) Samora Barros

GALE
CASTELLO

C. Aguas

Avenida do Ténis

Dr. Diogo Leote

Rua 1 de Decembro

T. C. Aguas

⑩

Albufeira
Beach

Rua Latino Coelho

④
⑥

Rua Padre Semedo

FERREIRA

Av. 5 de T Outubro

①

③ ⑤

Av. da Liberdade

Tunnel to beach

Praça
Republica

Town Hall

Rua Joaquim Pedro

Largo Enghenheiro
Duarte Pacheco

⑦

Old
Village

Rua Cândido dos Reis

Rua Alves Correia

0   50   100 m

Rua José Bernadino da Batera

②

⑧ ⑨

⑫ ⑪

Av. 25 de Abril

Rua dos Telheiros

Fisherman's
Beach

Rua C. Herculano

Largo Cais
Herculano

Fish Auction

Pier

PRAIA DE OURA
MONTECHORO

Rua Sacadura Cagral

MONTECHORO
OURA BEACH

Albufeira – old Moorish town

One of the liveliest resorts in the Algarve, Albufeira (pronounced 'Ahl-boo-fair-a') was called 'castle on the sea' by the Moors. The charm of the original fishing village has been preserved in the twists and turns of cobbled lanes, lined with pretty, whitewashed houses.

BEACHES

At the **Praia dos Pescadores** (Fishermen's Beach), local fishermen unload their catch, mend their nets and occasionally touch up the paint-work on their boats. There are fish auctions here from 0800–1000 daily. The main town beach, approached by a tunnel cut through the rock, is excellent for swimming and sunbathing but tends to become crowded. To the west are the smaller beaches of **São Rafael**, **Coelha** and **Castelo**.

THINGS TO SEE AND DO

Krazy Golf **
The wacky astroturf course is surrounded by subtropical gardens, ponds and lakes so pedalo rides are part of the fun. Other attractions include a Quad circuit, swimming pools and an exotic animal farm. *Krazy Golf is at Algoz, 30 mins from Albufeira, by car or bus. Open daily June–Sept 0930–2300, Oct–May 0930–1900.*

Parque do Território (Territory Park)
Scheduled to open shortly, this ambitious development will include an observatory and science and cultural centres. Ask at the Turismo for further details.

Zoomarine **
There are shows featuring dolphins, seals and parrots, as well as aquariums, swimming pools, a sea museum, cinema and funfair. *Zoomarine is at Guia, on the N125. Opening times and facilities depend on time of year. See your travel rep. or call 289 560300. www.zoomarine.com*

SHOPPING

The stalls set out each evening by the square are the nicest place to buy your souvenirs. If you are self-catering there's the fruit, veg and fish market on the main road to Montechoro (mornings only). If you don't get what you want, continue a little further to the large **Modelo** supermarket. The general market takes place around 2km (just over 1 mile) west of town on the first and third Tuesday of each month.

RESTAURANTS *(see map on page 34)*

The heart of the town's nightlife is the pedestrianised square of Largo Enghenheiro Duarte Pacheco, lined with restaurants and bars. On summer nights there is a carnival atmosphere here, with stalls lit by fairy lights selling arts, crafts and souvenirs and crowds of visitors thronging the narrow alleyways.

Adega Dom Pipas ££ ❶ Long-established popular Portuguese restaurant tucked in a tiny alleyway just off the main drag. Together with next door A Travessa, its outdoor tables create something of a street party atmosphere. *Travessa Dos Arcos. Tel: 289 588091. Open daily 1200– 1500 & 1800–2200.*

Anna's ££–£££ ❷ Set in a charming, ancient fisherman's cottage in the heart of the old town just above the beach, Anna's has been going strong for over 33 years, serving high-quality, delicious, adventurous, international cooking. *Rua Nova 7. Tel: 289 513558. Reservations tel: 91 7888211. Open daily 1800–late except Thurs.*

Atrium ££ ❸ Dine in grand, old-fashioned style upstairs in an old theatre hall enjoying *cataplana*, shellfish and steaks. Wednesday, Friday and Sunday are *fado* nights, but there is live music from Portugal, Africa and Brazil every other night. *Rua 5 de Outubro. Tel: 289 515755. Open daily 1830–2230.*

O Cabaz da Praia £££ ❹ If you want somewhere special for a romantic occasion, or just a top-class meal in an unbeatable clifftop location, it's hard to better this French-run, Michelin-listed restaurant. Superb French, international and Portuguese cuisine. *Praça Miguel Bombarda 7. Tel: 289 512137. Open 1200–1400 & 1900–2300. Closed Thur and Sat lunchtime.*

Cave do Vinho do Porto ££–£££ ❺ This is the only restaurant that we know of in the Algarve that actually celebrates the port of Portugal. It goes in the cooking and of course in glasses before and after the meal. Live music nightly. *Avenida da Liberdade 23. Tel: 289 589144. Open daily 1800–2300.*

O Dias £ ❻ Good value Portuguese grills on a small terrace with wonderful views. Book a seat as close to the clifftop as possible. *Praça Miguel Bombarda. Tel: 289 515246. Open 1200–1500 & 1800–2200. Closed Thur.*

Pampas Steakhouse ££–£££ ❼ This Argentinian-style restaurant occupies an attractive terrace on the corner of the main square and serves the best steaks in town. *Largo Enghenheiro Duarte Pacheco 53. Tel: 289 512320. Open daily 0900–0200.*

A Ruina ££–£££ ❽ Perhaps the most famous restaurant in Albufeira, A Ruina is a labyrinth of ancient rooms serving top-quality fish and shellfish. There is also a terrace overlooking Fishermen's Beach. *Rua Cais Herculano. Tel: 289 512094. Open daily 1230–1500 & 1900–2300.*

Tasca do Viegas £ ❾ Good, old-fashioned, rustic Portuguese *tasca* (traditional bar-restaurant), with a rooftop terrace, serving value-for-money meals in nice surroundings right by Fishermen's Beach. *Rua Cais Herculano 2. Tel: 289 514087. Open daily 1200–2300. Closed Sun.*

NIGHTLIFE

All the bars listed below are in Music Street (parallel to Fishermen's Beach).

Bizzarro ❿ Slightly Bohemian and nicely laid-back with live acoustic Brazilian guitar music every Tuesday. *Open daily 1200–late.*

Jo Jo's ⓫ Lively, friendly English-owned boozer with multiple television screens and football shirts pinned to the ceilings. Try and spot Gazza's signed England shirt! Fish and chips and Sunday roasts. *Open daily 1000–1600, 1830–late.*

7½ ⓬ If you fancy a change from Kiss (*page 41*), this is the place to be seen in the wee small hours in Albufeira old town. *Open nightly 2100–late.*

Montechoro and 'the Strip' –
bright lights and beaches

The inexorable spread upwards and outwards of what was originally the small fishing village of Albufeira has spawned the satellite resorts of what has been christened Nova Albufeira (New Albufeira). Just a couple of kilometres east of Albufeira Old Town, perched on the top of a hill, stands the resort of Montechoro, dominated by the landmark Hotel Montechoro. From here, the long, straight Avenida Sá Carneiro (known to everyone as 'The Strip'), lined with bars, restaurants and souvenir shops, descends all the way down to the lovely, if often crowded, beach of Praia da Oura. At the crossroads, around half-way down The Strip, the area's name changes from Montechoro to Areais de São João.

BEACHES
Further east are the small beaches of **Balaia** and the charming beach cove of **Olhos de Agua** (literally 'Eyes of Water'), so named for its rock formations. **Açoteias** is a small pine-shaded village next to the splendid golden 2km (1 mile) long beach of **Praia da Falésia**, backed by the easternmost cliffs in the Algarve.

TIP! Walk into Albufeira along the cliffs from Praia da Ouro. It's a lovely scenic walk. Time it to arrive at sunset, then you can enjoy the pretty sight of Albufeira's fairy-lit central market stalls.

Albufeira's Praia dos Pescadores (Fishermen's Beach)

SHOPPING

If you are self-catering, there's the **Marrachino** supermarket at the crossroads on The Strip but for more choice go to the large **Modelo** supermarket on the main road to Albufeira. For local colour continue on the same road to Albufeira's fruit, veg and fish market (mornings only).

RESTAURANTS

Os Compadres ££–£££ Attractive Portuguese restaurant with a traditional interior and a nice paved patio. An all-Portuguese menu including wild boar chops and an as-much-as-you-can-eat mixed grill special. *The Strip. Tel: 289 541848. Open daily 1200–1500 & 1800–2200.*

Fernando's Hideaway ££ Traditional welcoming country-style restaurant serving home-made Portuguese food. Don't be put off by the 'No Chips' sign (they are available on request!). *Brejos-Montechoro, 1km behind the Hotel Montechoro on road to N125, near Repsol garage (opposite side). Tel: 289 541618. Open Mon–Sat 1900–late. Closed Sun.*

MONTECHORO PARQUE

Next to the Hotel Montechoro, this small buzzing courtyard complex comprises several themed eating and drinking establishments. These include **Erin's Isle** (*see opposite*), **A Palmeira** (drinks and snacks), **The Taverna** (international/ Portuguese cooking), **Surf 'n' Turf Grill** restaurant, the **Swagman Bar**, **Don Corleone** (international/Italian dishes), **Casa dos Frangos** (The Chicken Shack), **Montechina** (Chinese food, eat in or take away) and **The Bread Shop** for fresh-baked local bread and cakes. There's also **Maxi-Mini Golf**, with 18 crazy holes for all the family.

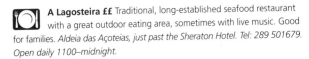

A Lagosteira ££ Traditional, long-established seafood restaurant with a great outdoor eating area, sometimes with live music. Good for families. *Aldeia das Açoteias, just past the Sheraton Hotel. Tel: 289 501679. Open daily 1100–midnight.*

Mumtaz ££ Traditional Indian restaurant offering excellent food and service. Shaded terrace and good-value children's menu. *Edificio Cristina, Montechoro (just off The Strip). Tel: 289 591445. Open daily 1800–midnight.*

O Poente ££ Smart traditional Portuguese restaurant with the atmosphere of the Algarve countryside. Grills are the speciality. *Brejos-Montechoro, 1km behind the Hotel Montechoro on road to N125 (by Repsol garage). Tel: 289 541419. Open daily 1100–2300.*

O Poeta ££–£££ Simple but stylish restaurant near the beach with an international menu featuring flambés and kebabs. *The Strip. Tel: 289 587520. Open daily 1700–2330.*

Yellow Submarine £ A friendly all-American diner, serving healthy portions at very reasonable prices. *The Strip. Open daily 1000–late.*

NIGHTLIFE

Erin's Isle Popular Irish bar and restaurant with live music nightly in the beer garden and in the air-conditioned bar. Snacks and full meals, plus imported beers and live sporting events on giant-screen TV. Children's play area. *Montechoro Parque, The Strip. Open daily 0930–late.*

The Garage Fun disco bar. *The Strip. Open daily 1800–late.*

Kiss Disco The Algarve's most famous and buzzing disco with regular theme nights. Entrance charge includes one free drink. *Rua Vasco da Gama, The Strip. Open nightly 2300–0600.*

Linekers Friendly pub atmosphere, with a party DJ every night, large screen TVs and an open-air terrace. *The Strip. Open daily 1200–0300.*

The marina – Vilamoura's focal point

Vilamoura – marinas and golf

This modern, purpose-built resort is one of the most popular in the Algarve. Low-rise apartment-hotels painted in pastel shades, broad tree-lined avenues and tastefully landscaped parks and gardens lead to the marina, the focal point where every conceivable amenity can be found.

The marina at Vilamoura is the largest in Portugal with berths for up to 1500 yachts. Boats leave from the quayside to explore the fascinating Algarvian coastline, with its myriad coves, beaches and unusual rock formations – some yachts will take you as far as Portimão and back. Big-game fishing (blue shark, tuna and record-breaking black marlin) is also popular while the watersports on offer include scuba diving, water-skiing and windsurfing. The marina is a place for people-watching, window shopping or promenading, especially at night when the entire harbour is illuminated. Souvenir outlets and chic boutiques alternate with smartly turned out cafés and terrace restaurants, offering everything from pizzas and pancakes to chow mein and chicken *piri-piri*. Karaoke is a popular form of entertainment in the family-friendly bars, which stay open well into the small hours.

The *Condor de Vilamoura*, a handsome replica of a 19th-century fishing schooner, takes passengers on half- or full-day excursions along the coast and on romantic evening cruises. Children under six travel free and the price includes a barbecue lunch on a remote beach.

THINGS TO SEE AND DO

Cerro da Vila *
Vilamoura means 'Moorish village' but the town's origins date back to Roman times. A new museum has been built around the remains, which include a villa, a farm and baths, and displays the coins, mosaics and other artefacts found here. *Avenida Cerro da Vila. Tel: 289 312153. Open daily 1000–1300 & 1700–2330. Admission fee.*

Golf
Vilamoura's four courses will appeal to experienced golfers and novices alike. The refurbished Old Course (number 1) has testing narrow fairways laid out between umbrella pines. Pinhal (number 2) has beautiful sea views, while the bunkers and water hazards of Laguna (number 3) present plenty of challenges. Recently opened is the Millennium course (number 4).

Roma Golf Park: If you're not quite up to the Old Course at Vilamoura, try this excellent little crazy golf course themed to the Roman finds next door at the Cerro da Vila museum. Two lots of 18 holes surrounded by fountains and pools. Tournaments for seniors and juniors on Sundays. *Open daily 1000–midnight.*

Health and fitness

The Rock Garden is a state-of-the-art sports centre with indoor and outdoor swimming pools, squash and tennis courts, Turkish bath, full size snooker tables, table tennis, darts, a gym and a fitness suite. *Aldeia do Campo, Vilamoura. Tel: 289 322740.*

Horse riding

For lessons with qualified, English-speaking instructors and hire of equipment, contact **Horses Paradise** in Almancil, which claims to be the longest-established riding centre in the Algarve, and specialises in leading small groups through beautiful countryside. *Tel: 289 394189.*

Tennis

Vilamoura Ténis is a high-quality facility offering lessons, tournaments and 12 courts for hire (five floodlit). *Vilamoura Ténis Centre. Tel: 289 302369.*

RESTAURANTS

Akvavit £££ Typical of the cosmopolitan nature of the marina, this very highly rated restaurant cooks mostly French and Portuguese dishes but do look out for its Swedish specials. Classy but informal surroundings. *Marina de Vilamoura. Tel: 289 380712. Open 1030–2330: lunch 1200–1600, dinner 1900–2230/2330.*

Chez Carlos ££ Family-friendly restaurant in the Almond Tree Park holiday complex offering Portuguese and international dishes and English breakfast. *Tel: 289 321432. Open daily 0900–late.*

CJ's ££–£££ Restaurant in the tranquil Old Village specialising in fish dishes, steaks and roast suckling pig. Tourist menu. *Tel: 289 388358. Open daily 1000–late.*

Mayflower ££–£££ The smart green and yellow shades and tablecloths set the scene for a fine meal on the waterfront. International menu. *Marina de Vilamoura. Tel: 289 314690. Open 1200–1500 & 1800–2300.*

 19th Hole £–££ Friendly Portuguese-managed English-style pub with Satellite TV and a nice position right in the corner of the marina. It dispenses English beers, full meals, snacks and kebabs as well as traditional Portuguese dishes. *Marina de Vilamoura. Tel: 289 301113. Open daily 0900–0200.*

 Normandia ££ Smart French-owned bar-crêperie right on the marina front, boasting over 80 different brands of beer and 40 types of whisky. The house speciality is their French-style grilled chicken. *Marina de Vilamoura. Tel: 289 313686. Open daily 1000–0100.*

 Ruis Bar ££ Bar and restaurant set just back from the marina offering Anglo-international food and drink to the homesick with live bands most nights. *Pateos da Marina. Tel: 289 312457. Open daily: bar 1800–0200, snacks and meals 0900–2300.*

NIGHTLIFE

Casablanca Enjoy live bands, disco and karaoke in a relaxed atmosphere. *Parque das Amendoeiras. Tel: 289 322680. Open daily 1800–late.*

Casino de Vilamoura American roulette, French roulette, Portuguese dice, Black Jack and 320 slot machines are just some of the dangers to your wealth in this classy establishment. *Tel: 289 302999. Casino open daily 1600–0300. Dinner 2030, Las Vegas-style show 2230. Passport required.*

TIP! Look out for the photographs of the world-record black marlin strung up Jaws-fashion on the dockside. It weighs around 737kg (equivalent to ten people or so!), measures some 3.65m (more than 12ft) long and was caught in 1993 from a Vilamoura-chartered boat.

Locals watch the world go by

Quarteira –
seaside and gypsy market

Once a typical Algarvian fishing village, Quarteira
(pronounced 'Kwer-tay-rah') has become a fully
fledged seaside resort, complementing its neighbour,
Vilamoura, but with a distinctive Portuguese flavour.
There are miles of golden sand stretching, almost
without interruption, to Vilamoura in one direction
and Vale do Lobo in the other. Shopping, restaurants
and bars are concentrated around Avenida Dr Francisco
Sá Carneiro, while watersports, golfing, tennis and
other leisure amenities are all within easy reach of
the resort.

THINGS TO SEE AND DO

Atlantic Park **
Atlantic Park has all the thrills and spills usually associated with waterslides and tunnels, plus showers, loungers, a snack bar and a children's pool. In the summer there's the added attraction of special family holidays. Atlantic Park is on road N125 (special buses run from here to Quarteira). *Tel: 289 397282. Open daily 0930–1830. Closed in winter. Admission charge.*

Horse riding
The farm at Quinta Dos Amigos, just outside Quarteira, has a riding centre with qualified, English-speaking instructors. Riding lessons are available and there are organised rides into the countryside and along the beach. Facilities also include two swimming pools, one for children. *Tel: 289 393399.*

BEACHES
A leisurely stroll along the promenade is the best introduction to Quarteira's beach area, with its varied selection of waterfront bars and restaurants, specialising in such succulent seafood dishes as *cataplana*. Fishing is still a way of life here: the auctioneers sell off the catches in the fish market to the west of the beach. Artificial sea defences keep the water calm here and the beach is well provided with sun-loungers, umbrellas, windbreak screens and pedalos.

SHOPPING
Quarteira's **gypsy market** (held every Wednesday) on the east side of town, is one of the largest and most colourful in the region. Fruit and vegetables are the mainstay but you'll also find clothes, towels, tablecloths and souvenirs, often at bargain prices – try bartering here. For more conventional shopping head for the pedestrian precinct leading into Rua Vasco da Gama.

RESTAURANTS

 Adega do Peixe ££ Reasonably priced seafood restaurant specialising in charcoal-grilled Portuguese dishes. *Avenida Infante de Sagres. Tel: 289 388370. Open 1000–midnight.*

 O Búzio ££ Tucked away around the corner from the fish market, but highly regarded for its good-value fish and seafood dishes. Occasional live music. *Largo das Cortes Reais. Tel: 289 315725. Open Mon–Sat 1200–1500 & 1930–2230. Closed Sun.*

 La Cabane ££–£££ Good French food. *Rua do Levante. Tel: 289 313819. Open daily 1900–2200.*

 Caravela ££ Smart, large, modern restaurant decorated in traditional style, specialising in monkfish, meat *cataplana* and seafood rice. *Largo do Mercado 17. Tel: 289 312280. Open Tues–Sun 1215–1500 & 1915–2200. Closed Mon.*

 Dallas £–££ Grilled Portuguese dishes and chicken to take away. *Fado* every Sunday. *Avenida Dr Francisco Sá Carneiro. Tel: 289 313293. Open daily 1200–1500 & 1900–midnight.*

O Infante ££ Portuguese restaurant on the promenade offering sea views, shellfish, grills and regional dishes. The speciality is *cataplana* (fish stew). *Avenida Infante de Sagres 131. Tel: 289 313576. Open 1000–midnight.*

The Joker ££ A long-established English-style pub restaurant serving a wide variety of dishes, from pasta to chicken *piri-piri*. Sunday roasts are available (lunchtime and evening sittings) and there are vegetarian and children's menus available. Satellite TV. *Rua Gonçalo Velho 13. Tel: 289 380267. Open Tues–Sun 1000–midnight, lunch Wed & Sun only 1200–1430, dinner Tues–Sun 1830–2200.*

O Koala £ Delicious and inexpensive *cataplana* or chicken *piri-piri* in the heart of Quarteira. *Avenida Carlos Mota Pinta Lot 116A. Tel: 289 314514.*

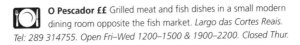 **Mr Pickwick's £** Standard English dishes, such as fish and chips, Cornish pasties and chips, sausage and mash, mixed grill and ploughman's lunch are served in this welcoming bar-restaurant. There's a children's menu and Satellite TV for entertainment. *Rua Abertura Mar. Tel: 289 388572. Open daily 1000–midnight.*

Mona Lisa's £ English restaurant and bar offering snacks as well as main meals. Menu includes beans on toast, bacon butties, steak and kidney pie, fish and chips, baked potatoes and steaks. Giant-screen Sky TV. *Rua Abertura Mar. Tel: 289 301721. Open 0900–after midnight (dinner served from 1800).*

O Pescador ££ Grilled meat and fish dishes in a small modern dining room opposite the fish market. *Largo das Cortes Reais. Tel: 289 314755. Open Fri–Wed 1200–1500 & 1900–2200. Closed Thur.*

Romeu ££ Friendly little backstreet place, plain but serving only authentic home-made fresh Portuguese cuisine, mostly seafood. *Rua Gonçalo Velho 40. Tel: 289 313990. Open 1200–1500 & 1900–midnight.*

NIGHTLIFE

D'Artagnan's Typical local bar with bingo, karaoke and live music during the week. *Rua Abertura Mar. Open 0900–after midnight.*

Hero's English bar serving a good selection of food, including English breakfasts, curries and Sunday lunch, with quiz nights and Sky Sports by way of entertainment. *Rua Bartolomeu Dias 33. Open Fri–Wed 1100–2200. Closed Thur.*

Vale do Lobo golf course

Vale do Lobo and Quinta do Lago –
golfer's paradise

Vale do Lobo (pronounced 'Val doh *Lobo*') and Quinta do Lago (pronounced '*Keen*ta doh *Lah*go') are two of the Algarve's most exclusive and prestigious resorts. Here, among pine forests and salt-water lakes, are the villas of Portugal's rich and famous as well as four championship golf courses, miles of golden sand, some of the best sports facilities in the Algarve and a good selection of bars, restaurants and nightclubs.

The watersports centre at Lake Side (Quinta do Lago) offers pedalos, kayaks, canoes and rowing boats as well as water-skiing. Experts are on hand for lessons in windsurfing and sailing. There are fishing trips on the lakes.

 The church of São Lourenço, just outside Almancil, is one of the few to survive the 1755 earthquake. It is decorated from floor to ceiling with the magnificent blue-glazed tiling known as *azulejo* (*see page 6*). The church is kept locked but a caretaker lives next door and will open it up for you between the hours of 0900 and 1800. (Please note that the church is closed over lunch 1300–1430.)

THINGS TO SEE AND DO

Fitness
Facilities at **Barringtons** include a golf academy, with floodlit driving range and instruction, squash courts, cricket nets, a fitness centre, sauna and jacuzzi. *Vale do Lobo. Tel: 289 398881.*

Horse riding
Paraíso dos Cavalos (Horses' Paradise) is one of the best riding centres in the Algarve. Boots and jockey caps are provided, as are lessons for beginners. Full-moon rides in summer. *Tel: 289 394189. Closed Mon.*

Karting
The **Almancil Karting Circuit** was inaugurated by the late great Ayrton Senna and is a replica of the Jacaregaguá Formula 1 circuit in Brazil. Independent circuit suitable for children aged 4 and over. *Almancil. Tel: 289 399899. Open daily from 1000.*

Tennis
The **David Lloyd Club** is owned by the former British International. The 12-court complex offers coaching and tournament matches. *Vale do Lobo. Tel: 289 366991.*

Watersports
Watersports Levanta organises a whole range of activities both on the lake and on the sea. *Quinta do Lago. Tel: 289 394929.*

GOLF COURSES

● **Pinheiros Altos:** the first 9 holes of the 'Tall Pines' par 72 course are set, as the name suggests, in attractive woodland, while the back 9 present some challenging water hazards. *Tel: 289 359910.*

● **Quinta do Lago:** designed by Henry Cotton, the two 18-hole par 72 courses feature lakes and challenging bunkers. The Portuguese Open has been held here on seven occasions. *Tel: 289 390700.*

● **San Lorenzo:** exclusively for the use of guests at the Dona Filipa and Penina Hotels, this par 72 course is currently rated No 2 in continental Europe. *Tel: 289 396534.*

● **Vale do Lobo:** a scenic course with clifftop views over the Atlantic. The famous 7th hole on the yellow loop involves a long drive across two ravines. Three 9-hole loops. Par 36+36+35. *Tel: 289 393939.*

RESTAURANTS AND BARS

 Bistro des Z'arts £££ Top-quality French/international food in a relaxed bistro setting. *Almancil. Tel: 289 395114. Open Mon–Sat 1200–1500 & 1800–2300. Closed Sun.*

 Bobby Jones Bar and Grill £££ Trendy eatery with views of the golf course. *Vilar do Golf, Quinta do Lago. Open 1800–midnight.*

 O Favo ££ A quiet, formal atmosphere pervades in this pub with a good location by the sea. *Praça Shopping, Vale do Lobo.*

 Iberico ££–£££ Good food in elegant surroundings in this popular Portuguese restaurant. Reservations essential. *Almancil (Vale do Lobo road). Tel: 289 394066. Open 1800–2230.*

 Julia's 1 ££–£££ The best place for beachside drinks and dining, Julia's is renowned for its excellent seafood and secret recipe African rice. *The original is at Praia do Garrão, its younger sister, Julia's 2 (Barca Velha), is on the beach at Vale do Lobo. Tel: Julia's 1 289 396512, Julia's 2 289 393939 ext 5416. Both open daily 1000–midnight.*

Memories of China £££ Ken Lo's famous Chinese restaurant. Try the sizzling three-seafoods platter. *David Lloyd Tennis Centre, Vale do Lobo. Open 1800–midnight.*

 Pequeno Mundo £££+ Serious dining for special occasions with classic international cuisine in a tranquil setting. *Almancil. Tel: 289 399866. Open Mon–Sat 1800–2300. Closed Sun.*

 Pig and Whistle ££–£££ No, this is not yet another Brit-pub but a smart family-run restaurant and bar, known throughout the region for its first-class international cooking. *Old EN 125, Almancil. Tel: 289 395216. Open Mon–Sat 1830–late. Closed Sun.*

 Rovers Return £ Traditional English pub serving Sunday roasts, steak and kidney pies, etc, with children's menu. *Rua da Republica, Almancil.*

 Rumours £ English-style bar with all Sky Sports channels, providing a great atmosphere in which to watch live events. Snacks. *Rua da Republica, Almancil.*

 T Club £££ The place to be seen for people with expensive tastes. *Buganvilla Plaza, Quinta do Lago.*

 The Teapot £–££ Nice spot for a traditional afternoon cuppa, with a pretty garden-terrace in which to relax. Also serves lunches, including a Sunday roast. *Almancil. Tel: 289 393625. Open Tues–Sun 1100–1800. Closed Mon.*

 ## SHOPPING

Apolonia Supermarket Well-stocked English-style supermarket with a good selection of wines and spirits. *Rua 5 de Outubro, Almancil.*

Florida Golf Everything for the golf course. *Rua 5 de Outubro, Almancil.*

Griffin Bookshop English-language fiction and non-fiction, second-hand, children's books and ordering service. *Rua 5 de Outubro 206-A, Almancil. Tel: 289 393904.*

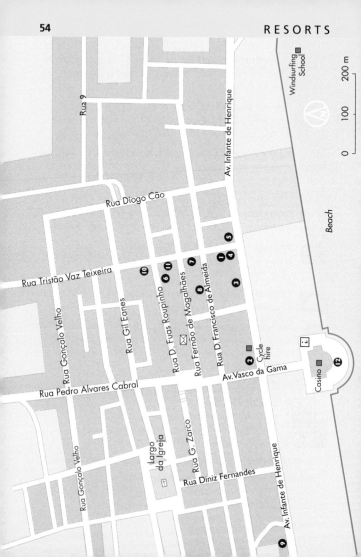

Windsurfing School

Beach

0 100 200 m

Rua 9

Av. Infante de Henrique

Rua Diogo Cão

Rua Tristão Vaz Teixeira

Rua Gonçalo Velho

Rua Gil Eanes

Rua D. Fuas Roupinho

Rua Fernão de Magalhães

Rua D. Francisco de Almeida

10 **6** **11** **7** **1** **4** **5**

8 **3**

2 Cycle hire

Av. Vasco da Gama

Rua Pedro Alvares Cabral

Largo da Igreja

Rua G. Zarco

Rua Diniz Fernandes

Rua Gonçalo Velho

Casino **12**

Av. Infante de Henrique

9

Monte Gordo – endless beach

People think 'big' in Monte Gordo: the beach is vast, the hotels and apartments are in high-rise blocks, while – for big spenders – there is a casino on the promenade. Popular with Spanish families, who cross the border to enjoy the lower prices, Monte Gordo is a lively resort with disco-clubs, karaoke bars and restaurants offering folk dancing and *fado* evenings.

The main reason for coming to Monte Gordo is the beach – 20km (12.5 miles) of shimmering sand, backed by pine forests and citrus orchards and stretching as far as Praia Verde, Alagoa and Manta Rota. For watersports enthusiasts, the off-shore lagoons are perfect for sailing, water-skiing and windsurfing while the seawater temperatures here are the highest in Portugal.

The stately 18th-century town of Vila Real de Santo António, only 3km (1.8 miles) away, makes a pleasant change from sea and sand. It was laid out on a grid plan by the Marquês de Pombal, famous for redesigning Lisbon after the Great Earthquake of 1755. Most visitors stop for lunch (shellfish is the local speciality) before making the short border crossing to Spain. The road bridge linking Vila Real de Santo António to its Spanish counterpart, Ayamonte, was completed in 1991; alternatively there are ferry crossings at 40-minute intervals.

 Not everything in Monte Gordo is modern – take a tour of the town in an old-fashioned pony and trap, leaving from the sea front by the Hotel Vasco da Gama (summer afternoons only).

THINGS TO SEE AND DO

Cycling
Bicycle hire is available from Fernandos at daily or weekly rates. *Guadiana Shopping Centre, Avenida D. Infante Henrique. Tel: 281 513881.*

Jeep safaris

Join in a one-day jeep convoy and explore the inland region. *Ask your rep for details.*

Sea fishing

The *Blue Emerald* – a 33-footer – takes beginners and experienced anglers on deep sea and big-game fishing trips. *Ask your rep for details.*

SHOPPING

The shops in the Guadiana Shopping Centre and on Avenida D. Infante Henrique cater for most visitors' needs:

Carvela: nice pottery and glassware, locally made candles and mugs. *Avenida D. Infante Henrique.*

Marrachino: supermarket with an excellent range of port, as well as fresh bread. *Avenida D. Infante Henrique.*

Other places to try are:

Casa Caravela: good selection of crystal. *Rua Dr Teófilo Braga, Vila Real de Santo António.*

Ourivesaria: Portuguese jewellery, gold and silverware. *Rua Dr Teófilo Braga, Vila Real de Santo António.*

RESTAURANTS AND BARS (see map on page 54)

 Cabana ££ ❶ A steak house is a novelty in this land of fishermen; the house speciality however is shrimps in a spicy sauce! *Rua Bartolomeu Perestrelo. Tel: 281 511845. Open 1200–late.*

 Copacabana ££–£££ ❷ Swordfish steaks, sardines, pork kebabs, etc, are grilled on a huge barbecue in the courtyard of this promenade restaurant. *Avenida D. Infante Henrique. Open 1100–midnight.*

 O Dourado ££ ❸ This restaurant, with a shady beach terrace, offers a wide range of traditional Portuguese dishes. Its speciality is a whole range of *cataplanas. Avenida D. Infante Henrique. Tel: 281 512202. Open 1000–late.*

Goa ££ ❹ An Indian restaurant with a difference. For the uninitiated a supplementary menu explains the ingredients which provide the distinctive Goan taste. *Rua Fernando Pó. Tel: 281 512606. Open 1800–late.*

Ipanema £–££ ❺ Home-baked baguettes, cakes, pastries and ice-creams served under straw beach parasols. *Avenida D. Infante Enrique. Open 1000–late.*

John's Bar £–££ ❻ English-style pub in the centre of town, with happy hours from 2000–2300. *Rua de D. Fuas Roupinho. Open 1200–late.*

Mr Bee's £–££ ❼ Snug British bar-restaurant serving traditional British home cooking in a friendly atmosphere. *Rua Tres. Open daily 1000–late.*

Nox Bar £–££ ❽ A stylish bar with resident DJ. *Rua Francisco de Almeida. Open 2200–late.*

Paddy's Irish Bar £–££ ❾ Lively karaoke bar with happy hour from 2000 to 2200. *Avenida D. Infante Henrique. Open daily 2000–late.*

Pizzeria La Mamma ££ ❿ A busy Italian restaurant in the centre of town offering excellent salads and pasta dishes as well the usual variety of pizzas. *Rua Tristão Vaz Teixeira. Tel: 281 542865. Open 1100–late.*

Rendezvous £ ⓫ Diners eat to the accompaniment of pop or *fado* music in this friendly Anglo-Portuguese bar-restaurant. Dishes include vegetable or steak pie and chips, chicken *piri-piri* and lasagne. *Rua Tristão Vaz Teixeria. Tel: 281 542569. Open 1000–2300.*

NIGHTLIFE

Casino de Monte Gordo ⓬ The newest casino in the Algarve, with gaming rooms, floor show and restaurant. *Tel: 281 512224.*

Sagres and Cape St Vincent

The small fishing port of Sagres (pronounced 'Sah-gresh') lies just a few kilometres from Cape St Vincent, where fierce westerly winds sweep in from the Atlantic, sending the sea crashing against the rocks. It's an area of quite stunning natural beauty with pristine, surf-washed beaches backed by towering cliffs and dunes. Apart from watersports, visitors can look forward to bracing coastal walks, fishing trips, boat trips and jeep safaris.

Standing on Sagres Point, a bleak promontory to the west of the town, is the Fortaleza (Fortress). It was built in the 15th century and its forbidding grey walls once contained Henry the Navigator's famous school of seamanship. From here there are several ways to reach the Cape: by boat (cruises leave from the fishing harbour), by car (via the EN268) or on foot – the clifftop walk is exhilarating, with fabulous views along the coast and out to sea.

On the way is the 17th-century Fortaleza do Beliche, restored in the 1960s. Cape St Vincent, mainland Europe's most westerly point, was 'the end of the world' until Vasco da Gama, Magellan and other Portuguese explorers opened up the maritime routes to Africa and America. From the top of the lighthouse it's a 60m (200ft) drop to the hazardous rocks below. The souvenir stalls at the Cape do a brisk trade in chunky, hand-knitted fishermen's sweaters.

TIP! Watching the sun set over the Cape is an unforgettable experience whatever the time of year; but in spring and autumn, there's the added pleasure of seeing huge numbers of migrating birds winging their way over the cliffs.

Traditional Portuguese tile work

THINGS TO SEE AND DO

Boat trips

Boats depart daily for Cape St Vincent and magnificent views of the windswept Costa Vicentina. The round trip takes approximately two hours. Fishing excursions (first-timers and experienced anglers welcome), including shark fishing, are also on offer, usually departing daily 1630 – the round trip takes approximately three hours. Catches include sea bass, bream, squid, and mackerel. Ground fishing is also available if you give at least 48 hours' advance notice. *Contact Turinfo, tel: 282 620003 for all boat trip details.*

Fortaleza **

Only the chapel and the castle walls survive from the small town built here by Henry the Navigator. Climb the battlements for superb views of the Cape, then take a look at the Rosa do Ventos (Wind Rose), a stone dial 43m (140ft) in diameter, thought to have served as a mariner's compass.

Fortaleza do Beliche **

The original fortress was destroyed by Sir Francis Drake in 1587 in an operation designed to forestall the Spanish Armada. Overlooking the sea is an attractive, white-domed chapel dedicated to St Catherine.

Lighthouse **

Visitors may be allowed to climb the lighthouse tower to inspect the twin 1,000-watt lamps, visible for up to 90km (56 miles) and among the most powerful in Europe. Up to 200 ships navigate the busy shipping lanes every day. Opening times are at the discretion of the lighthouse keepers.

BEACHES

There are four good beaches near Sagres. The largest, and most sheltered, is **Praia do Martinhal**, near Baleeira and the Windsurfing Club. Closer to the village is **Praia da Mareta** (Sagres Point). **Praia do Tonel** is good for surfing while **Praia do Beliche** is an excellent sandy beach but is vulnerable to strong westerlies. Sailboards and mountain bikes can be hired.

THE COSTA VICENTINA

Jeep safari convoys head for the beautiful, unspoilt west coast (*contact Turinfo, Praça da República, Sagres, tel: 282 620003*). Many of the magnificent beaches, backed by dunes and sheer cliffs, are accessible by car. Take the EN268 from Sagres to Vila do Bispo and the left turning to Praia do Castelejo where the moors behind the cliffs are covered in wild flowers.

Alternatively, continue along the main road to the tiny village of Carrapateira and the nearby beaches of Amado and (perhaps the most spectacular of all) Bordeira.

RESTAURANTS

 O Batedor ££ Excellent seafront location and varied menu, including peppered steak, grilled sardines and Portuguese steak. *Avenida das Naus, Baleeira. Tel: 282 924810. Open daily 0800–late.*

 Bossa Nova ££ Friendly restaurant with terrace, serving pizzas, pastas, vegetarian dishes, meat and seafood dishes, and fresh fish. Children's menu. *Rua da Mareta, Sagres. Tel: 282 624566. Open daily 1200–midnight.*

 O Pescador ££–£££ Quality seafood restaurant specialising in Portuguese dishes, such as *cataplana* (fish stew) seafood rice and grilled swordfish. *Rua Comandante Matoso, Baleeira. Tel: 282 624192. Open daily 0800–2200.*

NIGHTLIFE

Polvo Dreams Lively international bar with snooker tables, dart boards, video games and giant screen satellite TV. *Rua da N.S. da Graça, Sagres. Open daily 1800–0400.*

Topas Disco in the centre of town playing live rock and pop through the night. *Near the Parque de Campismo. Open daily 2300–0600.*

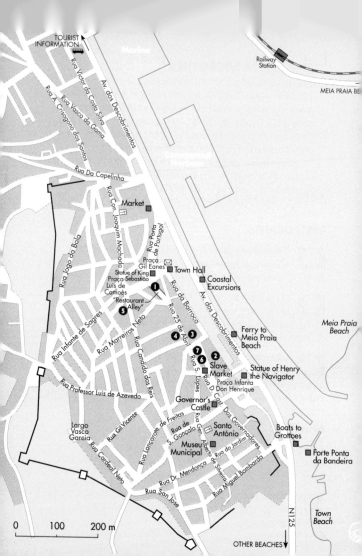

TOURIST
INFORMATION

Marina

Railway
Station

MEIA PRAIA BEACH

Rua Victor da Costa Silva

Rua A. Crisogono dos Santos

Rua Vasco da Gama

Av. dos Descobrimentos

Rua Da Capelinha

Rua Con. Joaquim Machado

Market

Rua Porta de Portugal

Rua Jogo da Bola

Praça
Gil Eanes
Statue of King
Praça Sebastião
Luis de
Camoès

Town Hall

Coastal
Excursions

"Restaurant
Alley"

Rua da Barroca

Av. dos Descobrimentos

Rua Infante de Sagres

Rua 25 de Abril

Rua Marreiros Neto

Rua Candido dos Reis

Ferry to
Meia Praia
Beach

Meia Praia
Beach

Rua S. Lopes

Slave
Market

Statue of Henry
the Navigator

Praça Infanta
Don Henrique

Rua Professor Luis de Azevedo

Governor's
Castle

Largo
Vasca
Garcia

Rua de
Gonçalo

Rua Lançarote de Freitas

Rua Gil Vicente

Rua Cardeal Neto

Santo
António

Rua Gen. Alberto da Silveira

Rua Dos Governadores

Rua do Jardim

Boats to
Grottoes

Forte Ponta
da Bandeira

**Museu
Municipal**

Rua Dr. Mendonça

Rua San José

Rua Miguel Bombarda

Town
Beach

N125

0   100   200 m

OTHER BEACHES

Lagos – harbour, fortress and picture-postcard beaches

Lagos (pronounced 'Lah-gosh') is an attractive town with a colourful past and plenty of good restaurants, shops, churches and museums.

Lagos' most famous former resident, Henry the Navigator, is commemorated by a statue in Praça Infante Dom Henrique. In the corner of the square is an arcaded building where African slaves were once bought and sold; it is now used for art exhibitions. The massive gateway at the bottom of Rua Miguel Bombarda forms part of the city walls, dating from the 14th to 16th centuries while the rooftop of the Ponta da Bandeira fort (now a museum) just outside the city walls affords excellent views of Lagos' superb natural harbour. Prettily painted houses and cobbled courtyards characterise the area around Rua da Barroca, where restaurants also cluster. Praça Gil Eanes contains a controversial monument to King Sebastião, who was killed on an ill-fated crusading expedition to Morocco in 1578. Around the square is an extensive pedestrian precinct with bars, cafés and shops selling eye-catching local handicrafts and souvenirs.

THINGS TO SEE AND DO

Forte Ponta da Bandeira *
Lagos' tiny fortress dates from the 17th century. Inside are some archaeological finds, a small exhibition (in Portuguese only) on the Age of Discoveries, a chapel dedicated to St Barbara and the Taverna restaurant. The roof is an excellent vantage point to view the broad sweep of Lagos Bay. *Open daily 0930–1200 & 1400–1730. Closed Mon. Small admission charge.*

Museu Municipal **
Set behind the famous church of Santo António, this overlooked museum is an old-fashioned cabinet of curiosities including church and archaeological

treasures, animal foetuses in formaldehyde and a bizarre five-legged calf. *Small admission charge. Rua General Alberto de Silveira. Tel: 282 762301. Open Tues–Sun 0900–1230 & 1400–1700. Closed Mon and public holidays.*

Ponta da Piedade ★★

Boat trips depart from the Forte Ponta da Bandeira to visit these extraordinary marine grottoes – one of the most remarkable features of the rugged Algarvian coastline. The sunsets too are spectacular. Ask your holiday representative for further details, or just catch a boat by the fort.

Santo António ★★★

The lavishly decorated 'golden' chapel is one of the few to survive the earthquake of 1755. Coloured *azulejo* tiles decorate the lower walls of the baroque chapel; the remainder is covered with fantastic ornamental woodcarving and giltwork, featuring winged angels, cherubs and saintly warriors. *Rua General Alberto de Silveira. Open Tues–Sun 0900–1230 & 1400–1700. Closed Mon and public holidays.*

RESTAURANTS *(see map on page 62)*

On Rua Alfonso da Almeida, is a whole row of traditional Portuguese restaurants ❶ including **Chicken Piri Piri**, **O Cantinho Algarvio**, **Lusitano** and **Pouso d'Infante**. All are good-value, medium-priced places to sample authentic Algarve cooking.

Barroca ££–£££ ❷ Adventurous international cuisine in a relaxed convivial jazz-bar atmosphere. Rooftop terrace. *Rua da Barroca. Tel: 282 767162. Open daily 1830–2300.*

Casa Amarela £–££ ❸ Wicker chairs and glass tables beckon tired shoppers in for a very civilised cuppa at this quiet tearoom. *Rua 25 de Abril. Open Mon–Sat 1000–midnight, Sun 1000–1500.*

Dom Sebastião £££ ❹ Probably the town's most celebrated restaurant, fish and shellfish are the specialities of this smart, traditional establishment. Opt for a romantic evening inside rather than lunch outside. *Rua 25 de Abril. Tel: 282 762795. Open daily 1100–1500 & 1830–2230.*

SHOPPING

Olaria Nova features some of the best modern pottery in the Algarve with many inventive contemporary designs. It also includes some lovely traditional and ethnic clothing, shoes, accessories and jewellery. *Rua 25 de Abril.*

Casa de Papagaio, named after its resident parrots, is a fascinating Aladdin's Cave of architectural salvage (including large church Madonnas and cherubs) and second-hand bits and bobs. *Rua 25 de Abril.*

Fools and Horses £ ❺ English bar and restaurant with a menu including Sunday roast, cod and chips, and steak and kidney pie. British draught beers are on sale. Karaoke and quiz nights. Sky Sports TV. *Rua Barbosa Viana 7. Tel: 282 762970. Open daily 1000–late.*

Love Shack £–££ ❻ The town's best burgers, chilli con carne and extra juicy ribs served by friendly and enthusiastic British owners. *Rua da Senhora da Graça 12a. Tel: 96 6380438. Open daily 1100–late.*

Mediterraneo ££ ❼ The most inventive and interesting menu in Lagos. Vegetarians and vegans are well catered for in this friendly restaurant with a large terrace for alfresco dining. *Rua da Senhora da Graça. Tel: 282 768476. Open Tues–Sat 1800–2300.*

NIGHTLIFE

Most of the conspicuous drinking in Lagos is done at the end of Rua 25 de Abril where half a dozen bars (including **Shaker**, **Sins**, **Eddie's**, **Stones** and **Zanzi Bar**) cluster. Look up to see the most attractive of them all, **Bon Vivant**, with a Gaudí-inspired interior and a smart rooftop terrace. There is another cluster of bars and nightlife around Rua 1 de Maio and Rua Marreiros Neto.

Ferradura Excellent locals' bar run by a very friendly Portuguese owner who speaks perfect English. Cheap beer and good *petiscos* (snacks), including local sausage and shellfish. *Rua 1 de Maio 26A. Open Mon–Sat 1100–late. Closed Sun.*

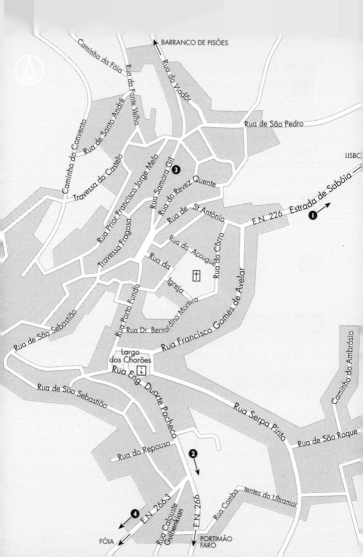

Monchique –
hill village and spa

The village of Monchique (pronounced 'Mon-sheek')
lies at the heart of the Serra de Monchique mountain
range. Its narrow cobbled streets climb steeply, lined
by traditional houses painted pastel shades of pink,
blue and green, old-fashioned gas lamps protruding
here and there from the upper storeys. The Serra is
also famous for its restaurants specialising in barbecue
lunches of spicy chicken *piri-piri*.

THINGS TO SEE AND DO

Caldas de Monchique **
Caldas is famous for its hot springs, long believed to have curative and
health-giving properties. Caldas itself is a lovely little village lying on the
edge of a densely wooded ravine, perfect for walking. Its beautiful old
casino building is now a gift shop but this is still a functioning spa and
(if you can stomach it) you can sample the original sulphurous spa water.
Better known, and much more palatable, is the spa water which is bottled
in the village and sold all over the Algarve. For something stronger, try
medronho, the local liqueur made from the berries of the local arbutus
('strawberry') trees.

Fóia **
At just over 900m (3000ft), Fóia is the highest point in the Algarve. There
are spectacular views of the coast, from Sagres and Cape St Vincent, in
the west, to Vilamoura, in the east. In the other direction, on a clear day,
there are views across the rocky plateaux to terraced hillsides planted
with eucalyptus, arbutus and cork oaks – sometimes even the mountain
ranges south of Lisbon may be visible.

TIP! **Walking**

Serious walkers should get hold of a copy of the Trilhos de Bio-Park Network Monchique map. It covers 300km (188 miles) of trails that are suitable for walking and mountain biking, all in Ordnance Survey detail. Another invaluable aid to serious walkers is *Landscapes of the Algarve* published by Sunflower Books. Both are on sale locally.

RESTAURANTS *(see map on page 66)*

Bica-Boa ££ ❶ Traditional inn on the Lisbon road, restored by Irish-Portuguese owners, with a wide range of regional and international dishes on offer. Outside terrace. *Estrada de Lisboa. Tel: 282 912271. Open daily 1000–midnight.*

O Caçador ££–£££ ❷ Needless to say, game is the speciality of the rustic Hunter restaurant, including boar, rabbit and partridge. *Quinta da Torrinha, Estrada de Monchique. Tel: 282 491878. Open daily 1200–1500 & 1800–2300.*

A Charrete £–££ ❸ Old wagon wheels are part of the décor in this attractive and friendly local restaurant. There's a reasonably priced tourist menu as well as a wide selection of regional specialities. *Rua Dr Samora Gil, Monchique. Tel: 282 912142. Open daily 1000–2200.*

Jardim das Oliveiras ££–£££ ❹ Lovely restaurant in a charming rustic setting just off the main road to Fóia. Chicken *piri-piri*, snails and hearty local meat dishes are the speciality. *Sitio do Porto Escuro, Monchique. Tel: 282 912874. Open daily 1000–late.*

Paraiso da Montanha £ ❹ Inexpensive regional cooking, including excellent chicken *piri-piri*. The restaurant is on the road to Fóia. *Estrada da Fóia. Tel: 282 912150. Open daily 1000–midnight.*

Quinta de São Bento £££ ❹ The perfect place to celebrate a special occasion, this traditional Portuguese restaurant has won several international awards and was once the summer residence of the Portuguese

Royal House of Bragança. Just as impressive are the views at nearly 900m (3000ft). *Quinta São Bento, Estrada da Fóia. Tel: 282 912143. Open daily 1200–late.*

Rampa £–££ ❹ Simple country restaurant with wonderful mountain views. While taking them in, try the tasty home-made soup, followed by chicken *piri-piri* and almond cake. *Estrada da Fóia, Samargal. Tel: 282 912620. Open daily 1100–late.*

Rouxinol ££–£££ ❷ The Scandinavian-run Nightingale is set in a delightful rustic hunting lodge and offers fondues, game (in season) and a good vegetarian choice. It's also open for coffee, snacks and home-made cakes. *Estrada de Monchique (opposite turning to Caldas de Monchique). Tel: 282 913975. Open Tues–Sun 1200–2200. Closed Mon.*

SHOPPING

Casa do Forno Typical Algarvian souvenirs and crafts. *Rua Dr Francisco Gomes do Avelar, Monchique.*

Casa da Praça Some less usual handicrafts and souvenirs and an ideal starting point to look for that elusive gift. *Praça Alexandre Herculano, Monchique.*

O Descansa Pernas Portuguese *artesanato* (handicraft shop) specialising in cork, pottery, leatherware and souvenir ornaments. *Estrada de Sabóia, Monchique.*

O Poço Beautiful cork ornaments; also hand-decorated pottery. The shop is on the road to Fóia. *Estrada da Fóia.*

Thick winter woollies may be the last thing on your mind down on the sunbaked coast but it's cool and windy at Fóia and good-quality hand-knitted cardigans and pullovers are always on sale here.

Ardecor High-quality handicrafts, clothing and accessories, wooden toys, pottery and lovely hand-painted wooden furniture. *Largo dos Chorões (opposite main square).*

Portimão – shopping and sardines

A busy port on the River Arade, Portimão (pronounced 'Porteemow') is also the largest shopping centre in the Algarve. Many of the 19th-century houses here have painted tile façades and fine wrought-iron balconies and the main squares too are attractive; Largo 1 de Dezembro, for example, is a garden square with tiled benches depicting episodes from Portuguese history.

SHOPPING

Portimão's gift and souvenir shops are concentrated in the area bordered by Largo 1 de Dezembro, Praça da República and the parish church. Handicraft exhibitions are often held in the Old Market. If you're bargain hunting, look out for unusual items of jewellery like stone necklaces, or bracelets made with freshwater pearls.

THINGS TO SEE AND DO

Arade Cruise **
Take a trip up the Rio Arade aboard an old-fashioned Portuguese 'gondola' (a traditional, brightly painted, high-prowed vessel, nothing like the Venetian type!) to the beautiful town of Silves (*page 75*).

Boat trips **
Boats from Portimão make the trip both east and west along the most picturesque Algarve coast between Armação de Pêra and Lagos. If you choose a half-day trip, you will head east past the glorious beach coves surrounding Carvoeiro. Algar Seco is a curiosity of old sea caves, with dramatic arches and grottoes, now completely dry. Then it's on past strange towering rock formations, with names such as 'the elephant', 'the ocean liner', or, if you go towards Lagos, 'King Kong'! Your boat will also explore small caves coloured green, yellow and purple by mineral deposits, barely big enough to enter.

Ferragudo**

On the opposite side of the estuary from Portimão is Ferragudo, a village where people instinctively reach for their cameras. This quaint little village, where time seems to have stood still, is noted for its typically Portuguese architecture, with a strong hint of Moorish influence. Just beyond the village is the *fortaleza* (fortress), which stands on the excellent beach of Praia Grande. Bearing an uncanny resemblance to a giant child's sandcastle, it stands opposite the Fortaleza Santa Catarina in Praia da Rocha and together they once controlled this harbour. The Ferragudo fortress is now in private hands and is not open to the public.

The harbour at Portimão

LARGO DA BARCA

This charming flower-filled square, next to the road bridge, and marked by a giant chimney, is reached by walking underneath the arches of the Sardine Dock. It is home to a clutch of Portimão's best restaurants. **Forte & Feio** (*tel: 282 418894*) and **Dona Barca** (*tel: 282 484189*) are two favourites but also highly rated is **Trinca Espinhas** (*tel: 282 418854*). All are open daily and serve top-quality Portuguese dishes with an emphasis, naturally, on the fruits of the sea (all £££).

RESTAURANTS *(see map on page 70)*

Blarney Castle £–££ ❶ Portimão's liveliest bar – Irish, of course, with a good selection of draught beers. Live music nightly, and a menu featuring fresh salmon, fish and chips, steaks and grilled chicken. *Rua Damião L Faria e Castro. Tel: 282 414240. Open 1030–late.*

The Haven ££ ❷ This Anglo-Portuguese combination is an old favourite serving grilled sardines, chicken *piri-piri*, liver and onions, curries, fruit crumbles and vegetarian dishes. *Rua João Annes. Tel: 282 426272. Open Mon–Sat 1130–1500 & 1830–2130. Closed Sun.*

Kibom ££ ❸ Situated in a street full of restaurants, Kibom is housed in a typical one-storey Algarve house and specialises in fish and shellfish. *Rua Damião L Faria e Castro. Tel: 282 414623. Open daily 1100–1600 & 1800–2300.*

Sambal £ ❹ A menu with a difference, featuring the cuisine of Bali, Malaysia, Timor and Thailand. Try the *rijsttafel* – a banquet of 14 small dishes, enabling you to sample a wide range of unusual oriental flavours – or simple soup and satay at bargain prices. Vegetarian dishes also available. *Rua de Santa Isabel 14–16. Tel: 282 422072. Open Mon–Sat 1800–2200.*

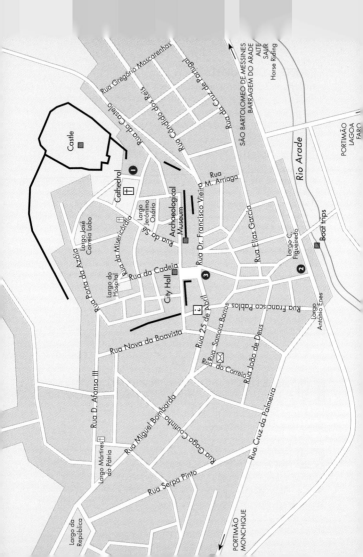

Silves – ancient Moorish capital

Modern visitors to Silves (pronounced '*Sil*-vesh') will find it hard to believe that this sleepy town was once the wealthy capital of a Moorish province. When the Arabs were finally expelled in 1242 the Christians returned, remodelling the castle and replacing the mosque with a cathedral. Today Silves is the centre of a prosperous farming region, the pretty, unspoilt villages surrounded by orchards producing oranges, lemons, figs and other fruit in abundance.

THINGS TO SEE AND DO

Arade boat trips **
Take an old-fashioned Portuguese 'gondola' on a 90-minute trip to Portimão (*page 71*), along the River Arade, which was once the highway that brought fabulous riches to Silves. *Trips Mon–Sat. Tel: 282 424243 for reservations/details.*

Castle ***
The network of 13th-century battlements and turrets is still largely intact, though heavily restored. From the parapets the views of the Arade Valley are spectacular. In the flower-filled castle courtyard are traces of an Arab palace, built by the last Moorish ruler of Silves. The courtyard is also said to be haunted by an enchanted Moorish girl. This sylph-like figure is said to appear at midnight on Midsummer's Eve as she awaits the handsome prince who will one day break her spell. *Open daily 0900–1800. Admission charge.*

Cathedral *
Like the castle, Silves Cathedral dates from the 13th century and, despite a subsequent baroque facelift, the rib-vaulted choir and tombs of crusading knights are reminders of its medieval origins. *Open (summer) daily 0830–1830 – winter times vary. Donation expected.*

Fábrica do Inglês *

The 19th-century English cork factory has been converted into a museum with its own brewery and six restaurants. Every night at 2300 a street party with music and clowns is staged featuring *Aquavision* – a spectacular multimedia water and laser show. *Tel: 282 440440. Entrance free 0900–1800, admission charge 1800–midnight.*

Horse riding

Go trekking through some of the most beautiful countryside in the Algarve. Beginners and experienced riders welcome. *Vale Fuzeiros (near Messines). Tel: 282 332466.*

Municipal Archaeology Museum **

The museum, constructed around a 12th-century Arab well, has Bronze Age, Roman and Moorish items. *Rua das Portas de Loulé. Open daily 1000–1230 & 1430–1800. Admission charge.*

Torreão da Porta da Cidade **

The Turret of the City Gate is the last surviving inner city wall gate. This barbican was built in the 12th/13th century and for many centuries was home to the municipal council. Today it holds the municipal library. *Open Tues–Sat 0930–1300 & 1400–1730. Closed Sun–Mon. Admission free.*

Alte ***

Alte is one of the prettiest villages in Portugal, where seemingly every other house or balcony is wreathed in oleander, hibiscus and geraniums. The 16th-century church, decorated with blue and white painted *azulejos*, is also striking. Alte is renowned for its singing and folk dancing ensembles. *Call the Alte Turismo, tel: 282 478666 for more details.*

SHOPPING

Housed in a lovely 16th-century building near the castle is the **Estúdio Destra**, the studio and gallery of Kate Swift, an artist renowned for her hand-painted tiles and ceramics.

RESTAURANTS *(see map on page 74)*

Café Inglês ££ ❶ This Anglo-Portuguese venture, located in a charming old town house, has a perfect setting on the steps of the castle next to the cathedral. Everything from full Portuguese meals to coffee and delicious home-made cakes. *Castle Steps. Tel: 282 442585. Open Sun–Fri 1000–late. Closed Sat.*

O Cais ££ ❷ Riverside restaurant with traditional Algarvian décor, specialising in charcoal-grilled dishes, especially fish. *Rua José Estevão. Tel: 282 445202. Open for lunch and dinner.*

Casa Velha de Silves ££ ❸ Renowned, traditional Portuguese restaurant overlooking the main square. Regular concerts of *fado* and other folk music in the basement bar. *Rua 25 de Abril. Tel: 282 445491. Open daily 1100–1500 & 1800–2300.*

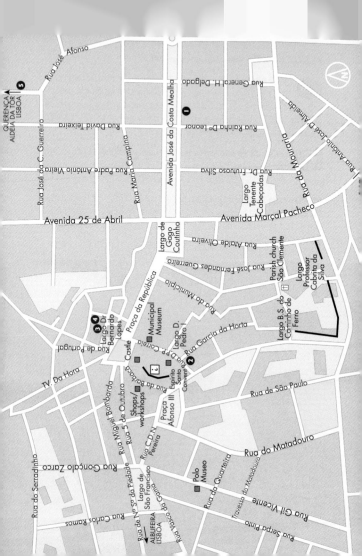

Loulé –
castle, churches and crafts

A busy little town famous for its gypsy market, Loulé (pronounced 'Loo-*lay*') is a flourishing centre of local handicrafts and one of the best places in the region to see artisans at work.

THINGS TO SEE AND DO

Castle **
Of Loulé's Arab fortress, rebuilt in the 13th century, only the walls remain. Climb the stone steps to the battlements for fine views of the town and the surrounding countryside. *Rua Paio Perez Correia. Open Mon–Sat 1000–1730.*

Church of Nossa Senhora da Conceição **
Across the street from the castle is the attractive 17th-century Church of Nossa Senhora da Conceição. The walls are decorated with blue and white tiles depicting scenes from the Life of the Virgin. *Rua Paio Perez Correia. Open Mon–Fri 1000–1200, Sat 1000–1400.*

Horse riding
An exciting way to see the local countryside with panoramic views, river crossings and sightseeing. Night rides with a barbecue are organised in the summer. Transport available. *Centro Hípico, Quinta do Azinheiro, Aldeia da Tôr. Tel: 289 415991.*

Municipal Museum **
Next door to the Tourist Information office, housed in the commander's residence in the old castle, is a small exhibition of Roman coins and pottery and a reconstruction of a traditional Algarvian kitchen. *Edifício do Castelo. Open Mon–Fri 0900–1730 & Sat 1000–1730.*

RESTAURANTS *(see map on page 78)*

Avenida Velha ££–£££ ❶ Long-established, well-known Portuguese restaurant specialising in fresh fish, including sole, swordfish, tuna, prawns and *cataplana* (fish stew). *Avenida José da Costa Mealha 40/Rua Rainha D. Leonor. Tel: 289 416474. Open 1200–1530 & 1800–2230. Closed Sun.*

Bicasvelhas £££ ❷ Highly rated Portuguese and international cooking served up in the oldest building in town. Reservations recommended. *Rua Martim Moniz 17/19. Tel: 289 463376. Open 1800–midnight.*

Casa dos Arcos ££ ❸ Traditional local cooking in a modernised century-old house with brick arches and pillars. Shellfish is the speciality. *Rua Sá de Miranda. Tel: 289 416713. Open Mon–Sat 1200–1500 & 1900–2200. Closed Sun.*

Paralelo 38 £–££ ❹ Plain and simple dining from a short menu in a traditional Loulé house. *Rua Sá de Miranda. No telephone bookings. Open Mon–Sat 1200–1500 & 1900–2200. Closed Sun.*

Restaurante de Querença £££ ❺ Game dishes, including rabbit and wild boar, are on offer in this lovely village restaurant in the foothills north of Loulé. Reservations recommended at weekends when there is live entertainment. *Largo da Igreja, Querença. Tel: 289 422540. Open daily except Wed, 1200–1500 & 1900–late.*

SHOPPING

There's a daily **market** in Loulé, in the Moorish-style building at the top of the main street, the Avenida José da Costa Mealha, but most visitors come on Saturday morning to see the colourful **Gypsy Market**. There's no shortage of gifts and souvenirs for sale (everything from handbags and *esparto* (sea grass) mats to painted roosters and ceramic plates), as well as an enormous range of food, including olives, spices, cheeses and jars of local honey.

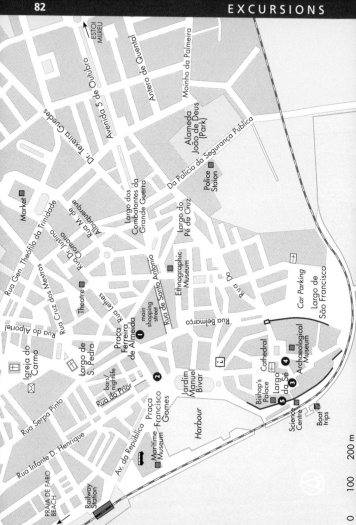

PRAIA DE FARO BEACH

Railway Station

Rua Infante D. Henrique

Rua Serpa Pinto

Igreja do Carmo

Rua do Alportel

Rua Gen. Theófilo da Trinidade

Market

Rua Dr. Justino Cromano

Rua Cruz dos Mestres

Rua M. Albuquerque

Theatre

Dr. Teixeira Guedes

Avenida 5 de Outubro

ESTOI MILREU

Antero de Quental

Moinho da Palmeira

Alameda João de Deus (Park)

Da Policia da Segurança Publica

Police Station

Largo dos Combatentes da Grande Guerra

Largo do Pé da Cruz

Largo de S. Pedro

Praça Ferreira de Almeida

Rua de Leitões

main shopping street

Rua de Santo António

Ethnographic Museum

Rua Belmarço

Rua de Sé

Jardim Manuel Bivar

Harbour

Praça Francisco Gomes

bars/ nightlife

Rua da Prior

Av. da República

Maritime Museum Francisco Gomes

Car Parking

Largo de São Francisco

Cathedral

Bishop's Palace

Largo da Sé

Archaeological Museum

Science Centre

Boat trips

1 main shopping street

2

3

4

5

0   100   200 m

Faro – Algarve's capital

The capital of the Algarve, Faro (pronounced 'Fah-roh') is a lively commercial centre and port with an authentic Portuguese atmosphere. There is half a day's sightseeing in the relaxed and peaceful Old Town, entered through the Arco da Vila, an imposing Italianate gateway commissioned by the bishop of Faro after the great earthquake had destroyed its medieval predecessor. The street beyond the arch leads to the spacious central square, with its cathedral and archaeology museum and streets lined with fine houses, decorated with wrought-iron balconies.

THINGS TO SEE AND DO

Archaeological Museum **

Housed in a beautiful restored convent, the Archaeological Museum has some fine Roman mosaics and a collection of rare medieval *azulejo* in the cloisters. *Praça Alfonso III, Old Town. Tel: 289 822042. Open Mon–Fri 0900–1230 & 1400–1700. Admission charge.*

Cathedral ***

The biggest attraction of this 13th-century building is the chance to climb its tower (68 steps) to enjoy great views over town and the lagoon. *Old Town, Largo da Sé. Open Mon–Sat 1000–noon & 1500–1700. Open Sundays only during services. Admission free.*

Centro Ciência Viva *

This 'Centre of Living Science' is a new hands-on discovery centre for children and adults. *Open July–mid Sept Tues–Sun 1600–2300; mid Sept–June Tues–Fri 1000–1700, Sat & Sun 1500–1900. Admission charge.*

Igreja do Carmo ***

It's a ten-minute walk from the city centre inland to the Carmelite Church with its macabre Capela dos Ossos, lined from floor to ceiling with the skulls and bones of more than 1,200 monks. *Largo do Carmo. Open 1000–1300 & 1500–1700.*

SHOPPING

Faro's shops are concentrated in the pedestrianised area around Rua de Santo António and Rua Vasco da Gama.

EXCURSIONS

Milreu **

These knee-high walls are all that is left of a 3rd-century Roman villa. The famous Dolphin mosaics are still in reasonable condition. *Signposted just before Estói. Open May–Sept Tues–Sun 0930–1230 & 1400–1800, winter closes at 1700. Closed Mon. Small admission fee.*

Palace of Estói **

This charming 19th-century palace is painted pastel pink, with bright blue *azulejo* staircases, classical statues, urns filled with flowers and a riot of bougainvillaea. Alas, only the gardens are open as the building is currently being restored to create a hotel. *Estói village. Open Tues–Sat 0930–1230 & 1400–1730. Closed Sun & Mon. Free admission.*

RESTAURANTS *(see map on page 82)*

Adega Dois Irmãos ££ ❶ The Two Brothers have been satisfying the palates of Faro visitors and locals since 1925 with superb fish and seafood. Atmospheric traditional tiled dining room. *Praça Ferreira de Almeida 25. Tel 289 823337. Open 1000–1600 & 1800–2300.*

Aliança ££ ❷ This traditional Portuguese café is one of the oldest in the country. Patrons have included prime ministers as well as the French writer, Simone de Beauvoir. *Praça Francisco Gomes.*

Mesa dos Mouros ££ ❸ Charming small modern restaurant housed in an ancient building next to the cathedral. Eat inside or out on the cobbled square. *Largo da Sé, Old Town. Tel: 289 878873. Open daily 0830–midnight.*

One of Faro's picturesque streets

Piri Piri do Costa ££ ❹ Traditional Portuguese restaurant serving shellfish, plus grilled meat and fish dishes. *Praia de Faro. Tel: 289 817442. Open Wed–Mon 1000–midnight.*

Taverna do Sé £ ❺ Lovely little traditional café-bar just around the corner from the cathedral, perfect for a morning coffee and cake to the sounds of classical music or jazz. *Rua do Trem, Old Town. Open daily 1000–late.*

Tavira's architecture

Tavira and Cabanas –
stately town, island beaches

Tavira is an elegant town and nicely complements the growing resort of Cabanas. The coast here fragments into a series of spits, lagoons and barrier islands, which together constitute the Ria Formosa nature reserve. The warm waters on the shore side of the sandbanks are excellent for swimming, while the Atlantic beaches provide just the right conditions for windsurfing.

Get your bearings in Tavira by climbing the cobblestone lanes leading off Rua da Liberdade to the ruined **castle** (*open Mon–Fri 0830–1730, Sat & Sun 0900–1730*). From the little garden within the walls there are good views of the estuary and town and it's possible to count some of the domes and spires of Tavira's 22 churches. Next to the castle is the Church of Santa Maria do Castelo, remarkable for its double bell tower and enormous clock.

THINGS TO SEE AND DO

Quinta da Avestruz Alegre (The Happy Ostrich Ranch) *
See ostriches from the egg to full size. Activities for children include a mini zoo (kangaroos, deer, llamas, goats and sheep), pedal carts, bouncy castle, an assault course and crazy golf. *Tel: 96 6308696. Open daily Mon–Sat from 1000, Sun from 1400. Apr–Sept closes 2000, Oct–Mar closes 1700. Moderate admission charge.*

Ria Formosa Natural Park **
A beautifully wild area of salt marshes and lagoons, this reserve stretches from Quinta do Lago to Cacela Velha, embracing some of the best beaches in the region. Ria Formosa is also the breeding ground of many species of wading bird. The **Visitors' Centre**, at Quinta de Marim (*1km from Olhão on N125*), provides a good introduction to the area. *Visitors' Centre open daily 0900–1230 & 1400–1700.* Four-hour **cycle tours** of the Ria Formosa reserve are available at Rent a Bike (*Rua do Forno 33; tel: 281 321973*). **Barcos do Pantanal** runs regular guided boats tours of the Ria Formosa, departing from Santa Luzia (*4km (2.5 miles) west of Tavira; tel: 281 323356 for details*).

BEACHES

Tavira beach can be reached by ferry from the Quatro Aguas jetty between May and October. Other beaches nearby include **Pedras da Rainha**, which has its own offshore sandbank, reached by boat or on foot at low tide, and **Santa Luzia** from where there is a footbridge to Tavira Island. An alternative to the ferry is a small railway that crosses the causeway from Pedras d'el Rei, near Santa Luzia, to **Praia de Barril and** the extensive beaches of Tavira Island.

RESTAURANTS

Cabanas:

Atmosfera £ A tiny beachfront bar offering excellent English breakfasts at good value prices. *Avenida 28 Maio. Open 0900–midnight.*

Cantino Algarvio £–££ Pub and restaurant in one, serving pepper steak, fish platter, *tapas*, and *paella* amongst its varied offerings. *Behind Piano Bar off Avenida 28 Maio. Open Fri–Wed 1800–late. Closed Thur.*

Copacabanas £–££ Seafront restaurant offering grilled fish and curry, steak-on-a-stone, plus children's favourites, such as burgers, pizza and lasagne. *Avenida 28 Maio.*

Dona Inês ££ Large family-friendly restaurant with an attractive terrace, serving fish and meat grills. *Cabanas–Tavira Road. Tel: 281 370801. Open Tues–Sun 1230–1500 & 1830–2230. Closed Mon.*

Pedros ££ Typical Portuguese restaurant, specialising in razor clams with beans, monkfish, *cataplana* and seafood rice. *Rua Capitão Batista Marçal 51 (by boats to beach). Tel: 281 370425.*

Piano Bar ££ Popular seafront restaurant serving English and international dishes. Children's menu and off-road patio. *Avenida 28 Maio 2. Open 1830–late. Closed Sun.*

Tavira:

O Canecão ££ 'The world's best *cataplana*' is the modest boast at this shellfish specialist. They certainly have a good number to choose from, including chicken and lamb. *Rua José Pires Padinha 162. Tel: 281 325260. Open Fri–Wed 1200–1500 & 1800–midnight. Closed Thur.*

Carmina £ Right by the fish market, this small dining room festooned with nets and traps is full to the gills with locals and fishermen when all others are empty. *Rua José Pires Padinha 96. Tel: 281 322236. Open daily 0900–2200.*

Imperial ££ An award-winning Portuguese restaurant. The *serrabucho de marisco* (mixed seafood with pork) is one of several dishes to be recommended. *Rua José Pires Padinha. Tel: 281 322306. Open daily 1100–late.*

Kudissanga ££ Fascinating menu comprising around a dozen dishes from the old Portuguese colonies of Angola, São Tomé e Principe, Guinea Bissau, Cape Verde Islands and Mozambique. Simple tiled dining room. *Rua Dr Agusto Silva Carvalho 8. No telephone bookings. Open daily 1900–late.*

O Patio ££–£££ Highly regarded rooftop restaurant, serving up an international menu with Portuguese specialities such as *cataplana* and fish kebab. *Rua Dr António Cabreira. Tel: 281 323008. Open 1100–1500 & 1800–midnight.*

Patrick's £–££ English-style pub with food, including home-made chilli, chicken *piri-piri* and various vegetarian dishes. *Rua Dr António Cabreira. Open 1800–late.*

Quatro Aguas £££ Very highly rated, smart attractive traditional fish and shellfish restaurant near the quay by the beach. *Quatro Aguas. Tel: 281 325329. Open Tues–Sun 1200–1530 & 1800/1900–2230.*

NIGHTLIFE

Bar Toque Good selection of music. Try some drinks from the 'flaming bomb' cocktail list. *Rua Almirante Cândido dos Reis 118, Tavira. Open 2100–0400.*

UBI The only disco-club in Tavira. Happy hour 2200–2300. *Fabrica, Balsense, Tavira. Open 2200–0600.*

Lisbon

One of the great historic capitals of Europe, Lisbon is also a port with an exciting, cosmopolitan atmosphere. Built on a series of hills at the estuary of the River Tagus, its many attractions include St George's Castle, the Belém Tower and the Jeronimos Monastery, the medieval Alfama quarter and the restaurants and *fado* clubs of the Bairro Alto.

It is possible to see a good deal of Lisbon and to catch something of the flavour in just a few hours. South of the main square, Praça Dom Pedro IV, is the bustling Baixa quarter. Rebuilt on a grid pattern by the Marquês de Pombal, following the Great Earthquake of 1755, each of the uniform neo-classical streets was assigned to a particular trade.

At the top of Rua do Ouro is the Elevador de Santa Justa, an extraordinary metal tower with a lift and viewing platform said, quite erroneously, to have been designed by Gustave Eiffel. Near the exit are the haunting Gothic ruins of the Igreja do Carmo.

An elaborate triumphal arch at the end of Rua Augusta opens out on to Praça do Comércio and the waterfront. From here the outlook across the harbour to the statue of Cristo Rei is impressive.

Lisbon's cathedral, the Sé, was founded in 1150 to celebrate the reconquest of the city from the Moors (*open daily 0900–1900*). An imposing Romanesque building, its twin crenellated towers give it a fortress-like appearance. The medieval tombs behind the altar commemorate prominent Portuguese noblemen.

Yellow signs point the way to the Castelo de São Jorge (St George's Castle), past a succession of steep, cobbled streets with washing hung out to dry on the balconies. The Moorish keep is now little more than a shell but there are superb panoramic views of the city from the formidable battlements and walls. The courtyard has been transformed into a beautiful tree-shaded garden, the air scented with flowers, the lawns and ponds inhabited by doves, peacocks, cranes and pelicans, pheasants and (the traditional guardians of the city) ravens (*open daily 0900–sunset*).

Belém

The Mosteiro de Jerónimos, one of Portugal's great religious monuments, lies a few kilometres west of Lisbon proper, in the waterfront district of Belém. Completed in 1551, the monastery has to be seen for the fantastic Manueline decoration on walls, columns and doorways: vines, creepers, wild beasts and nautical motifs. *Open Tues–Sun 1000–1700.*

RESTAURANTS

There are some delightful art nouveau cafés on Lisbon's main boulevard, Avenida da Liberdade, which runs between Rossío and Praça do Marquês de Pombal. If you're feeling adventurous and want a more 'old world' atmosphere, head for Alfama where the tiny, unpretentious restaurants specialise in fish. In the evenings, the action moves to Bairro Alto, a lively neighbourhood of densely packed, 17th-century houses with small, reasonably priced restaurants on almost every street corner.

 Café a Brasileira ££ One of the city's most famous old-style coffee houses. *Rua Garrett 120. Open daily 1000–late.*

 O Cantinho do Aziz ££ A family-run Mozambican restaurant located just east of Rossío, specialising in spicy meat and fish curries. *Rua de S. Lourenço 3–5. Tel: 21 8876472. Open Mon–Sat 1100–midnight.*

 Cervejaria de Trinidade ££ Nineteenth-century beer hall-restaurant, decorated with colourful tiles and high vaulted ceilings. Grilled seafood is the house speciality. *Rua Nova da Trinidade 20. Tel: 21 3423506. Open 1000–midnight.*

 **Vává £** A self-service cafeteria where you can eat in or take away. The choice of food includes pies, quiches, pizzas, pastries and cakes. *Avenida Estados Unidos de América 100. Tel: 21 7966761. Open all day.*

View to Lisbon's cathedral

SHOPPING

Markets: Lisbon's lively fish market (*open daily except Sun*) is behind Cais do Sodré station on the waterfront. Nearby is the equally colourful Ribeira market, selling meat, fruit and vegetables, flowers, spices and wine. On Saturdays the famous flea market (Feira de Ladra – literally, 'thieves' fair') opens early on Campo de Santa Clara in the picturesque Alfama district.

Sevilla – quintessential Spain in a day

Sevilla is the most Spanish of all Spain's great cities: the home of Carmen, the capital of *flamenco*, a bastion of bullfighting and with stunning architecture left from two great international expositions. Just 160km (100 miles) east of the Algarve, it's a hot ticket (around 40°C in July!) and just too good an opportunity to miss.

The Expo city

Many of Sevilla's most splendid buildings come from the Exposición Iberoamericana (Hispanic American Exhibition) of 1929 and the World Expo of 1992. As you enter the city you will pass many of these. The state-of-the-art 1992 structures occupy the island of La Cartuja across the Guadalquivir River, while the more popular 1929 pavilions line the main thoroughfares and reflect the colourful and romantic architecture of their host nations – Mexico, Bolivia, Guatemala, and so on. Many are now museums or government buildings. King of all is the Spanish pavilion in the Parque María Luis, which is supposedly a reconstruction of a medieval palace. There is no admission inside, but its courtyard, the Plaza de España, is a magnificent sweeping semicircular colonnade fronted by tiled benches, representing every province of Spain. Ornamental tiled bridges cross canals to reach it while horse and traps do a brisk trade.

Tips on *tapas*

If you visit Sevilla on an organised tour, you will be left on your own around midday to explore Sevilla for a couple of hours, so if you want to see any of its attractions you won't have time to sit down to a proper meal. There are all sorts of international options but why not go native and visit a *tapas* bar. *Tapas* are small Spanish snacks – a few common examples being *queso* (cheese), *jamón* (mountain-cured ham), *albóndigas* (meatballs), *tortilla* (potato pancake), *salchichón* (salami), *chorizo* (spicy sausage), *salade de pulpo* (octopus salad), *ensaladilla rusa* (Russian salad), *gambas* (prawns),

Sevilla – one of Spain's great cities

aceitunas (olives) and *boquerones* (marinated anchovies). *Tapas* are always on display so simply point if your Spanish isn't up to ordering. Share half a dozen or so between two of you, wash it down with a *copa* or two of *vinho* and you will enjoy a decent local lunch at a reasonable price.

Rather Moorish

Sevilla's greatest buildings are a legacy of the Golden Age of the Moors who held the city from 712 to 1248. The highlight is the Reales Alcazáres, a fortified palace adorned with the most magnificent plasterwork, tiles and coffered ceilings. Nearby is the Casa de Pilatos. Its name comes from a legend that the house was fashioned after Pontius Pilate's home in Jerusalem, but this may be taken with a large pinch of salt. Whatever, it is an absolutely beautiful place and usually very quiet too – you may even have it to yourself.

Santa Cruz

Santa Cruz was once the poor Jewish enclave but today its neat and quiet whitewashed streets with their iron grilles and red geraniums are almost impossibly pretty. If Walt Disney ever includes Spain in its World Showcase, it will look exactly like this.

The biggest Gothic church in the world

Sevilla Cathedral was built mostly in the 15th-century on the site of a mosque whose minaret partially survives today as the huge landmark bell tower known as the 'Giralda'. As you step inside you can't fail to be awed by its size – which indeed was the deliberate intention of its builders. It feels almost as if you have shrunk. It is a huge and sumptuous building and the fabulous main altarpiece (the world's largest) alone contains 2000kg of gold – testament to the fact that in the days of the *conquistadores* Sevilla was the main

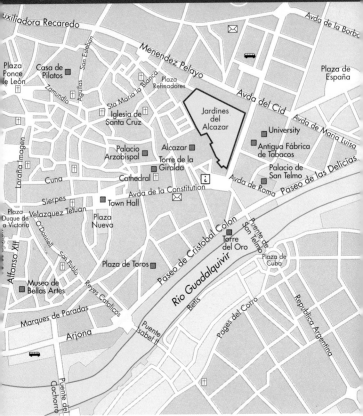

Spanish port. And, fittingly, the man who made the Spanish conquest of South America possible has left his mark here too. The Caribbean may claim the grave of Christopher Columbus but perhaps nowhere is more appropriate to his legacy than this awesome historic building right in the heart of Spain.

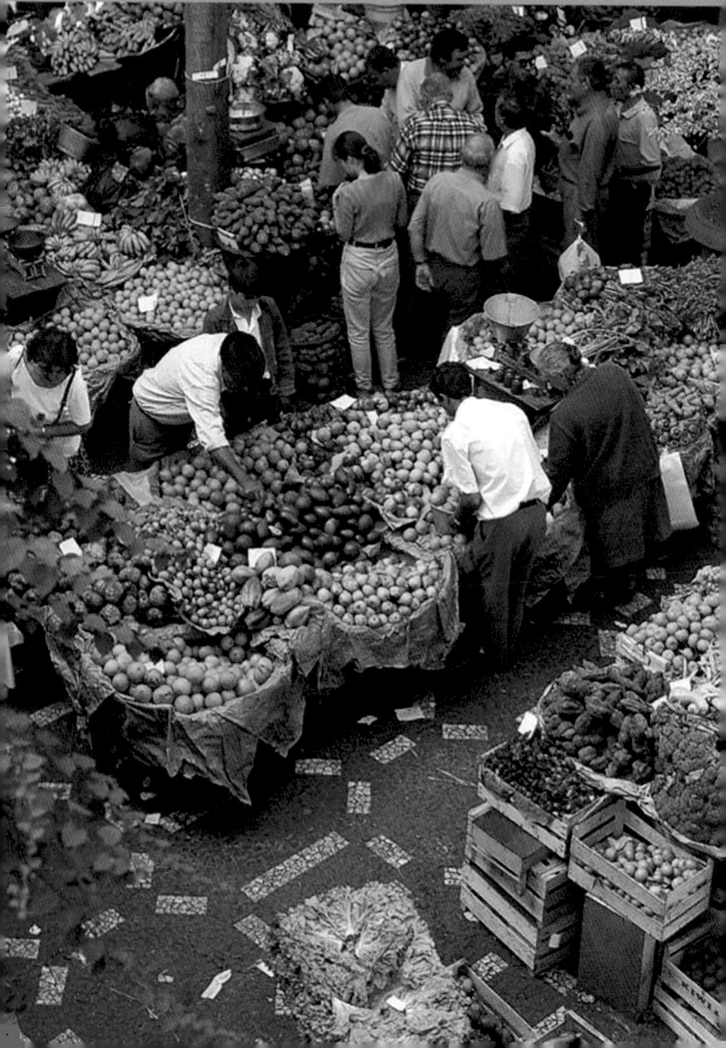

Food and drink

Soups
Usually made from fish or vegetables, soups make a nourishing, tasty and relatively cheap first course. Try *caldo verde*, made from shredded cabbage and potatoes, often served with thin slices of sausage, or *caldeirada de peixe*, a delicious fish soup similar to a *bouillabaisse*. Alternative starters include cured ham, prawn omelette and shellfish.

Bacalhau à brás
A Portuguese favourite, this consists of salt cod, shredded and fried with onions, garlic and potato.

Cataplana
This tasty seafood casserole takes its name from the copper vessel the food is cooked in. Apart from clams the ingredients usually include prawns, mussels and pieces of white fish steamed in their own juices, and pork and/or spicy sausage is often added. Servings of *cataplana* are usually for a minimum of two persons.

Fresh fish
A typically Algarvian dish, charcoal-grilled sardines are cheap and available everywhere, always served with fresh bread and boiled potatoes. The daily catch in most resorts includes tuna, swordfish, sea bass, bream, sole and red mullet. Most types of fish are simply grilled, but tuna may be cooked in a casserole with onions and peppers.

CHECKING THE BILL
In Portuguese restaurants, there is a small cover charge for bread and butter, which comes with olives, fish spread, and cheese. If you don't want these, say so. The Portuguese equivalent of VAT (called IVA) is usually added automatically to the bill and amounts to 12 per cent of the total. Tipping is at your own discretion, but 10 per cent would be appreciated.

Fresh fruit and vegetables abound at local markets

When ordering fish, check the price carefully – it may be calculated per kilo or *preço variável* (varying according to season and availability).

Meat dishes

Popular with tourists, chicken *piri-piri* is an African-influenced dish in which the chicken pieces are brushed with a chilli and olive oil sauce before being grilled. Steak or pork fillets are usually served in generous portions. *Bife à Portuguesa*, sirloin steak cooked with smoked ham and potatoes in the oven, is a succulent national dish. Also look out for *fígado com arroz*, liver and rice served in a tasty sauce, and *caldeirada de cabrita*, an appetising lamb or kid stew.

Desserts

Try to save room for one of the delicious Portuguese desserts, choosing from crème caramel, chocolate mousse, rice pudding, almond tart, or *queijo de figo* (layers of dried figs, ground almonds, cinnamon and chocolate).

DRINKS

Soft drinks

Citrus fruits are plentiful in the Algarve, though freshly crushed orange and lemon juice is surprisingly expensive (if you want fizzy orange or lemonade, ask the waiter for Fanta, Sprite or 7-up). The tap water is drinkable, but it is less palatable than the home-produced mineral water from Monchique.

PORT

Apart from the more common ruby and tawny port varieties, you'll come across a dry white port, served chilled as a delicious aperitif. Surprisingly, the Portuguese themselves are not great port drinkers.

COFFEE

The Portuguese are great coffee drinkers and there are
numerous ways of serving it:

- espresso-style black coffee is *um café* or *uma bica*.

- coffee with milk is *café com leite*.

- iced coffee is *café gelado*.

- regular black coffee is *uma carioca*.

- milky coffee, served in a glass, is *um galão*.

Wine

Portugal is a major wine-producing country and a bottle of wine with a
meal won't break the bank. Most restaurants will have an acceptable *vinho
da casa* (house wine). If you want red, ask for *vinho tinto*, if white, *vinho
branco*. *Vinho verde* (literally, 'green wine') is actually a youthful and slightly
sparkling wine, well suited to seafood.

Wine produced locally in the Algarve (look for the Lagoa label) tends to
be high in alcohol and a little on the rough side. Portugal's better vintages
are grown further north. They include Dão (similar to a Burgundy) and two
good-value wines from the Alentejo region, Borba and Redondo. If you're
in the mood for a celebration, try the Portuguese sparkling wine, *vinho
espumante*.

Beer and spirits

Sagres and Super Bock, two good-quality lagers, are the most popular
Portuguese brands. Many foreign beers are available in pubs or English-
style restaurant. The local firewater, *medronho*, is distilled from the fruit
of the arbutus tree. *Brandymel*, made with Portuguese brandy and locally
produced honey, is a sweet liqueur, like the delicious almond-based
amêndoa amarga.

Menu decoder

GENERAL

bica	espresso-style coffee
galão	white coffee (served in a tall glass)
chá	tea
pão	bread
manteiga	butter
queijo	cheese
vinagre	vinegar
azeite	olive oil
azeitonas	olives
pimenta	pepper
sal	salt
água (fresca)	water (iced)
gelo	ice
cerveja	beer
vinho (tinto/branco)	wine (red/white)
vinho de mesa/vinho de casa	table wine/house wine
prato de dia	dish of the day

TYPICAL PORTUGUESE DISHES

caldo verde	soup of mashed potato and finely shredded cabbage
sopa de marisco	seafood soup
caldeirada	fish soup with onions and potatoes
sopa de grão	chick-pea, tomato and onion soup
bacalhau	salt cod, cooked numerous ways: often with olives, garlic, onions and hard-boiled egg
bife de cebolada	steak braised in wine and onions
cozida portuguesa	a rich casserole of beef, pork, sausages, rice and vegatables

MENU ITEMS AND COOKING TERMS

On Portuguese menus, the dishes are often described very simply, with the main ingredient and the cooking method, as in *coelho assado* (roast rabbit). Here is a list of the commonest ingredients and cooking methods:

alho	garlic
almôndegas	meatballs
ameijoas	clams

arroz	rice
assado	roast
atum	tuna
besugo	bream
bife (also vaca)	beef
bolo	cake
borrego	lamb
caracóis	snails
cavala	mackerel
cebola	onions
chouriço	spicy sausage
coelho	rabbit
costeletas	chops
cozido	boiled
robalo	sea bass
estufado	stewed
favas	broad beans
feijóes	beans
frango	chicken
frito	fried
fumado	smoked
gambas	prawns
gelado	ice-cream
grelhado	grilled
guisado	stewed
lagostins	lobster
linguado	sole
lulas	squid
mariscos	shellfish
molho	sauce
nas brasas	braised
no forno	baked
peixe	fish
pescada	hake
pescadhina	whiting
polvos	octopus
porco	pork
presunto	cured ham
salmonete	red mullet
salsichão	salami
sobremesa	dessert
truta	trout
vitela	veal

Shopping

Markets

Every town of any size in the Algarve has a permanent covered market where local people shop (in preference to the supermarket) for inexpensively priced fruit, vegetables and fish. Larger markets also have stalls selling bread, cured ham, and local cheeses. Street markets are colourful affairs and you may pick up some bargains – ceramics, wicker baskets, lacework, linen, even old liquor stills. If you don't like the price, it's acceptable to barter.

Market days at a glance:

- Every Wed – Quarteira
- 1st Mon – Portimão
- 1st Fri– Sagres
- 2nd Tues – Alvor
- 3rd Mon – Silves
- Every Sat – Loulé
- 1st and 3rd Tues – Albufeira
- 1st Sat – Lagos
- 2nd Fri – Monchique
- 3rd Sat – Tavira
- 1st and 4th Sun – Almancil

Basketry

Basket weavers still work out of doors in the summer months. One popular spot is on the N125 near Boliqueime (for Loulé).

Ceramics, tiles and pottery

Among the most popular items are painted *gallos* (cockerels), inspired by a Portuguese folk tale. You'll also find miniature chimneys and brightly coloured jars and vases. *Azulejo* tiles – of the kind found in churches and other historic buildings – are only expensive if genuinely old. They are sold singly or in sets.

The best-known potteries in the Algarve are at Porches, where the speciality is floral-patterned *majolica*. Visit **Artesanato Reis** in Porches, to see the craftsmen hand-painting flowers, birds, fish and other motifs. *Open (summer months) Mon–Sat 0900–2000.*

Other pottery outlets are:
- Olaria Algarve, *N124, Alqueives, Porches (3km (1.8 miles) from Lagoa)*. Watch craftsmen at work. *Open Mon–Fri all day, Sat morning only.*
- Casa Algarve, *N125, Alqueives, Porches*. Sells locally produced pottery.
- Infante Don Henrique, *Rua Candido dos Reis, Albufeira*. Earthenware pottery.
- Domingos de Jesus Filipe, *N125, Penina, Portimão*. Traditional earthenware.
- Artesanato Regional Casa Matias, *Mercado Municipal, Tavira*. Traditional pottery. *Closed Sun.*

Copper and bronze

Bowls, trays, scales, small stills and lamps are made locally. The Caldeiraria Louletana, Rua da Barbacã, Loulé, is a workshop specialising in handmade brass and copperware.

Cork

Portugal is the world's largest exporter, and is famed for its cork products, ranging from place-mats, to whole sculptures. O Poco, Estrada da Foia, Monchique, sells a variety of cork items.

Take time to browse!

General arts and crafts outlets:

- **João Calado Earthenware**, cast iron, pottery, glazed tiles, cork and sconces. *N124, Torre, Lagos. Open daily.*

- **Arisol**, *Alporchinhos, Porches. Closed Sun.*
- **Porta da Moura**, *Rua do Repouso, Faro. Open daily 1000–2000.*
- **Estabelecimentos Sol Dourado**, *Rua Dr. Teófilo Braga, Vila Real de Santo António. Open Mon–Fri & Sat am.*
- **Aquário**, *Praça da República/Rua Vasco da Gama, Portimão. Open daily.*
- **Casa & Etc**, *Rua 5 de Outubro, Albufeira. Open Mon–Fri 1000–1300 & 1500–1900.*
- **Al Quatro**, *Estrada de Vale do Lobo, Almancil. Open Mon–Fri 1000–1300 & 1400–1900.*
- **Centro de Artesanato**, *Loulé.* Home-made rugs, ceramics, straw dolls, cork place-mats, palm-leaf items, lace shawls, *caravelles. Open daily.*

Traditional crafts on sale

- **Casa da Praça**, *Praça.* Wide range of handicrafts at reasonable prices.
- **Alexandre Herculano**, *Monchique. Open daily.*
- Try also the **Bazar Tânger**, *Rua José Pires Padinha, Tavira. Closed Sun.*

Handicrafts

Throughout the Algarve, shops specialising in *artesanato* sell typical Portuguese products, such as baskets, cork mats, lace tablecloths, woollen shawls, handmade rugs, brightly painted earthenware jars, copper lamps, confectionery, cockerels and *caravelles* (traditional sailing vessels made from wood).

Jewellery, gold and silverware

Portuguese craftsmen are famous for filigree – fine threads of gold or silver delicately interwoven to produce brooches and pendants, resembling birds, flowers or cockerels. *Marcasite*, a grey/black metallic mineral, was used in Moorish jewellery and is inexpensive.

For original jewellery:

● **Mogodor**, *Rua Gil Eanes, Lagos.*
● **Ingrid Serrão**, *Rua Direita, Portimão.*
● **Starte**, *Rua Guilherme Gomes Fernandes, Tavira.*
● **Allerbon**, *Marina, Vilamoura.*

Leatherware

Handbags, belts (often ornamented), wallets, purses, shoes and boots are all good value and generally of excellent quality. In Rua da Barbacã, Loulé, you can shop for leather belts and other items, and watch local artisans at work making saddles and harnesses.

Music

Take home a recording of *fado* music as a memento of your visit. Artists to look out for include Amalia Rodrigues, Carlos do Carmo and Madredeus.

Wines and spirits

Any large supermarket will have a large selection of wines and spirits. The best Algarvian wines carry the Lagoa label. Also look out for Borba, Redondo, Dão, the light wine known as *vinho verde* and quality wines from the Douro region. Port is widely available, either well known British brands like Croft and Cockburn or Portuguese labels, including Ferreira. Wine shops also stock varieties of *medronho* (arbutus berry liqueur), the delicious sweet liqueur made from almonds known as *amêndoa amarga*, and *brandymel*, Portuguese brandy blended with honey.

 Faro airport's departure lounge has a shopping arcade selling handicrafts drinks, tobacco, perfumes, regional sweets, cheeses, coffee, tea and delicatessen products, cameras, leather goods, books and stationery, and tapes and CDs. *Open 0700–midnight.*

Kids

The beautifully clean beaches of the Algarve are ideally suited to young families. Conditions at Praia da Rocha and Lagos are ideal for children learning to windsurf. Most resorts have pedalos for hire. The lakes at Quinta do Lago make a safe environment for pedalos, rowing boats, canoes, etc. There is also a children's playground here.

The Windsurf Centre at Meia Praia, Lagos runs 'Kids Days' (ages 9–16 only). The programme includes windsurfing lessons, volleyball, beach games and lunch – all under the watchful eye of a lifeguard. *The Watersports Centre, Lagos. June–Sept, Mon & Fri 1030–1600.*

Older children love boat trips

Boat trips

Day excursions leave from most resorts and older children will relish the adventure. Beware that younger children may get bored, however. It may also be a good idea to take a boat trip on your second week, when the children have acclimatised a little to the sun and heat. Boats explore the grottoes, as well as offering opportunities for swimming, diving and snorkelling.

Family restaurants

Most restaurants in the Algarve welcome children. Some even have high-chairs as well as children's choices on the menu.

Krazy World

Inland from Albufeira, this fun park, set in scenic surroundings, is well worth the half-hour trip. The attractions include crazy golf, a mini-zoo, crocodile shows, swimming pools, a Quad circuit and pedalos on the lake, plus bar, pizzeria and souvenir shop. *Algoz. Tel: 282 574134. www.krazy-world.com. Open daily May–Sept 1000–1930, Oct–April 1000–1800.*

Picnics

Picnics are worth considering if you're planning a drive, or a day out in the countryside. There are fully stocked supermarkets in all Portuguese resorts, but remember that most shops close for lunch – usually from 1300 to 1500. The local market is a much more interesting place to shop – here you will find fruit and vegetable stalls where you'll be able to buy the freshest produce (especially oranges, peaches and figs), as well as assorted local bread, sausages, cheeses and hams.

Waterparks

Ideal for children of all ages (and adults too!) it is easily possible to spend a whole day in one of the Algarve's waterparks. The biggest and best is Slide and Splash. However, this also gets very busy and Atlantic Park may be a quieter day for young families. Each has a number of amazingly convoluted slides with exciting names such as Corkscrew, Flying Carpet and Black Hole, as well as junior pools, snack bars and other amenities. Fully qualified lifeguards are always on hand. Private buses take customers to and from the resorts.

- Slide and Splash: *N125, Vale de Deus, Estombar, near Armação de Pêra.*

- Atlantic Park: *N125, Quatro Estrados, near Quarteira.*

- The Big One: *N125, Alcantarilha.*

Zoomarine

This spectacular attraction features dolphin and seal shows. Other amenities include aquariums, swimming pools, cinema, funfair, a bar and restaurant. *N125, Guia, near Albufeira. Opening times: see page 35.*

Family water fun

Sports and activities

Birdwatching

Local birdwatching trips can be organised through the tourist offices in Portimão and Lagos. *See page 11 for details.*

Cycling

Bicycles and motorbikes can be rented out by the day, from Motorent, at the following main resorts:
- Praia da Luz. *Tel: 282 788928.*
- Praia da Rocha, Hotel Rocha 2. *Tel: 282 416998.*
- Praia do Cavoeiro. *Tel: 282 356551.*
- Armação de Péra. *Tel: 282 356551.*

Fishing
- Cepemar, Portimão. Big-game fishing for Hammerhead shark, marlin, swordfish, *bonito* and 200 other species. *Tel: 282 425341.*
- Centro de Pesca da Quinta do Lago. Fishing on the salt-water lake. Prices include all fishing equipment. *See your rep for details and bookings.*

Horse riding
The following centres offer riding lessons for all age groups, including children, as well as refreshment and other facilities.
- Quinta dos Amigos. *Tel: 289 393399.*
- Vilamoura, Centro Hípico. *Tel: 289 322675.*
- Albufeira, Vale Navio. *Tel: 289 542870.*
- Lagoa Casa, Agrícola Solear, Porches. *Tel: 282 381444.*
- Portimão, Centro Hípico da Penina. *Tel: 282 415415.*

- Lagos, Tiffany's Riding Centre. *Tel: 282 697395.*
- Benagil/Carvoeiro, Casa Galaraz Riding Centre. *Tel: 282 658055.*
- Mexilhoeira, Grande Val de Ferro Riding. Free pick-up from Alvor, Praia da Rocha and Portimão. *Tel: 282 968444.*

Scuba diving

- Atlantic Scuba Diving (PADI affiliated), based at Praia da Aveiro near Albufeira offers courses for novices, expert and specialist divers. Daily equipment hire also available. *Tel: 289 587479.*
- Sea Sport Centre, Praia da Luz. Officially licensed diving school. Regular wreck and night dives organised. *Tel: 282 789538.*

Sport and fitness centres

- **Barringtons:** squash courts, gymnasium, cricket pitch with nets, snooker room, sauna and Turkish bath, indoor and outdoor swimming pools and, for golfers, putting green, pitching green, driving range and tuition option. Daily and weekly membership available. *Vale do Lobo.* Tel 289 396622.
- **Burgau Sports Centre:** tennis and squash courts, sauna, gymnasium, pool, table tennis, many other sports, swimming pool and children's playground. *Burgau.* *Tel: 282 697350.*
- **Rock Garden:** tennis and squash courts, gymnasium, indoor and outdoor swimming pools, snooker tables, table tennis and darts. *Vilamoura.* *Tel: 289 322740.*

Tennis

Racquet hire as well as tuition are available at the following centres:

- Vale Do Lobo, David Lloyd Tennis Centre. *Tel: 289 393939.*
- Vilamoura, Rock Garden (*see opposite*).
- Carvoeiro Rocha, Brava Tennis Club. *Tel: 282 357847.*
- Burgau Sports Centre (*see opposite*).
- Vilasol Tennis Centre. *Tel: 289 300525.*

Walking

The Algarve Walkers Club organises local rambles. *Tel: 282 449098.*

Festivals and events

Festivals and fairs
Algarve Events is a brochure published in several languages by the regional tourist authority (available from local tourist offices, in hotels, etc) giving up-to-date listings of cultural events.

January
January 1–6: carol singing in the local villages.

February
Carnival all over the Algarve in the weekend before Shrove Tuesday. Loulé Carnival is the biggest and best, with colourful floats, bands and dancers. Eggs, flour and other substances are hurled about so visitors are advised to wear protective clothing! *More details from the Casa de Cultura, tel: 289 463900.*

March
March 20: Alvor holds its annual *feria* with entertainment including live music and traditional *fado* performances.

April
Throughout the Algarve there are religious processions in the lead up to Easter, especially on Palm Sunday and Good Friday.

May
May 1: May Day folk festival: traditional singing and folk dancing, with food and drink on sale, celebrated in Alcoutim, Albufeira, Alte, Monchique. International Film Festival: Portuguese and foreign films shown in cinemas in Alvor, Lagoa, Lagos, Loulé, Vilamoura and Albufeira. *Tel: 289 800400.*

June
International Music Festival, promoted by the Gulbenkian Foundation, the biggest celebration of its kind in the Algarve, with concerts, ballet and other performances by world famous orchestras and artists in a number of centres, including Albufeira and Silves. *Tel: 289 800400.* Tavira 'Saints Festivities' – music, dancing and processions in the specially decorated streets. *Tel: 281 322511.*

July

Tavira Jazz Festival involving local and international artists and musicians. *Tel: 281 322511*. Alcoutim Handicraft Festival on the wharf by the Guadiana River; also celebration of regional gastronomy – game and freshwater fish. Silves Beer Festival – a celebration of local Portuguese beers, with tastings, in the grounds of the castle, plus brass band concerts and folk dancing. *Tel: 282 442255*. Faro – Feira do Carmo handicraft festival. Faro Motorbike Festival – bike convention with rock music. *Tel: 289 803604*.

August

Lagoa 'Fatacil' country fair, embracing handicrafts, tourism, agriculture, commerce and local industry. The entertainment includes live bands, craft exhibitions, food and wine tasting, shows, exhibitions and competitions. *Tel: 289 800400*. Tavira – folk dancing shows and concerts of *fado*, folk and classical music are held in the gardens throughout the summer. *Tel: 281 322511*. August 11: Cabanas 'Fish Festival', with market, live bands, dancing and *fado* music. August 29: Banho de 29 in Lagos – fireworks and live music on the local beaches. *Tel: 082 763031*.

September

National Folklore Festival, a showcase for traditional Portuguese folk music and dancing, with groups performing from all over the country. Various venues, culminating in the final competition, held on the beach at Praia da Rocha. *Tel: 289 800400*. Portimão International Photographic Exhibition. *Tel: 282 419131*. Lagoa Wine Festival, with tastings, to promote the local varieties and vintages. Monte Gordo 'Nossa Senhora das Dores', annual fair with games, side shows, folk concerts and other musical entertainment. After Monte Gordo the fair moves on to Tavira. *Tel: 281 322511*.

October

Choirs Festival – concerts by choirs from all over the Algarve. *Various venues*. *Tel: 289 800400*. Monchique Country Fair – exhibition of local handicrafts.

December

December 8: ceremonial blessing of the crib in many churches.

Taking better holiday photos

All professional photographers know that it's not the camera that takes good pictures, it's the photographer. David Bailey takes stunning pictures using a cheap throwaway camera, and we all know the show-offs with the expensive lenses who still cannot take a decent picture. The truth is that camera technology is now so good that anyone can take top-quality pictures, if you follow a few simple rules.

Choose the correct film for the lighting conditions: film stock is available in different speeds depending on the lighting conditions. 100 ASA is best for the bright light you will experience at most resorts, where the brightness of the sun is enhanced by reflections from the sand and water. 400 ASA is better for indoor photography or anywhere that you would need to use flash – for architectural shots in shade, for example. If, like most photographers, you want to take a mix of indoor and outdoor pictures, buy an intermediate speed of film – 200 ASA is ideal.

Use light to your advantage: everybody knows the golden rule that you should never take a picture directly into the sun – ideally the sun should be behind you, so that the light falls where you want it – on the subject of your photograph. But all rules can be broken to advantage: shooting into the sun can be used to create a back-lit effect, whereby the sun creates a silhouette around the subject – even more effective at sunset.

Use shadows: the opposite of sunlight is shadow, and many professional photographers prefer to take pictures early in the day, when the sun is low and the shadows are deep, rather than during the main part of the day, when every detail is equally lit. Shadows enhance the details of sculpture and architecture: even a boring wall can become an interesting subject if shadows enhance the texture.

Think about photo composition and a central focus for your shot

Avoid the harsh light of the hottest part of the day: another reason for avoiding harsh sunlight is that it has the effect of bleaching colour; that is why the blue sky looks white on your photographs, and why intensely coloured flowers look pale and washed out. The best time for photography is early in the morning and later in the afternoon, in the soft magical hours before dusk. If you do take photos during the day, wait for the sun to go behind a cloud, which helps to diffuse and soften the harsh light.

Get up close to your subject: the big mistake that every amateur photographer makes is to try and cram too much into the picture. Good photographs are ones that choose a detail that stands for the whole. Take a picture of a stone sculpture, rather than the whole of the church façade; of a single orchid rather than the whole of the flower-filled meadow; of a water-filled rockpool rather than the whole sweep of beach.

Catch the family unawares: try to avoid the obvious pose when taking pictures of your friends and family. Better still, try to avoid posing them at all – candid photographs (those that are taken without the subject being aware) are often far better than posed ones, because the subject is relaxed and looks more like their normal selves, rather than wearing an artificial smile or a cheesy grin. Take pictures of your family as they eat, shop and fool around – bringing life and movement into the photograph.

Tell a story: ask yourself, as you compose the picture, what is this picture about and will it interest another person? Think like a photo journalist as you look for picture subjects that will arouse curiosity and make the viewer want to take a second look. You want people to say, as they look at your pictures, 'that is interesting', not 'what a bore!'.

And finally … use a reputable film-processing company. Don't trust your precious holiday pictures to any old express film-processing service, or the investment you have made in good-quality film stock and careful composition will be thrown away. If in doubt, wait until you get home before having your pictures developed, and use a processor whose standards you know and trust.

Think about both foreground and background

Preparing to go

GETTING THERE

The cheapest way to get to the Algarve is to book a package holiday with one of the leading tour operators. Tour operators specialising in the Algarve offer flight-only deals or combined flight-and-accommodation packages at prices that are hard to beat by booking direct.

The Algarve's sandy beaches stretch for miles

If your travelling times are flexible, and if you can avoid the school holidays, you can find some very cheap last-minute deals using websites. You should also check the *Travel* supplements of the weekend newspapers, such as the *Sunday Telegraph*, and the *Sunday Times*. They often carry adverts for inexpensive flights, as well as classified adverts for privately owned villas and apartments to rent in the Algarve.

BEFORE YOU LEAVE

Holidays should be about fun and relaxation, so avoid last minute panics and stress by making your preparations well in advance.

It is not necessary to have inoculations to travel in Europe, but you should make sure you and your family are up to date with the basics, such as tetanus. It is a good idea to pack a small first-aid kit to carry with you containing plasters, antiseptic cream, travel sickness pills, insect repellent and/or bite relief cream, antihistamine tablets, upset stomach remedies and painkillers.

Sun lotion can be more expensive in the Algarve than in the UK so it is worth taking a good selection especially of the higher factor lotions if you have children with you, and don't forget after-sun cream as well. If you are taking prescription medicines, ensure that you take enough for the duration of your visit – you may find it impossible to obtain the same medicines in Algarve. It is also worth having a dental check-up before you go.

DOCUMENTS

The most important documents you will need are your tickets and your passport. Check well in advance that your passport is up to date and has at least three months left to run (six months is even better). All children, including newborn babies, need their own passport now, unless they are already included on the passport of the person they are travelling with. It generally takes at least three weeks to process a passport renewal. This can be longer in the run-up to the summer months. For the latest information on how to renew your passport and the processing times call the Passport Agency on 0870 521 0410, or access their website www.ukpa.gov.uk

You should check the details of your travel tickets well before your departure, ensuring that the timings and dates are correct.

If you are thinking of hiring a car while you are away, you will need to have your UK driving licence with you. If you want more than one driver for the car, the other drivers must have their licence too.

MONEY

You will need some currency before you go, especially if your flight gets you to your destination at the weekend or late in the day after the banks have closed. Traveller's cheques are the safest way to carry money because the money will be refunded if the cheques are lost or stolen. To buy traveller's cheques or exchange money at a bank you may need to give up to a week's notice, depending on the quantity of foreign currency you require. You can exchange money at the airport before you depart. You should also make sure that your credit, charge and debit cards are up to date – you do not want them to expire mid holiday – and that your credit limit is sufficient to allow you to make those holiday purchases. Don't forget, too, to check your PIN numbers in case you haven't used them for a while – you may want to draw money from cash dispensers while you are away. Ring your bank or card company and they will help you out.

INSURANCE

Have you got sufficient cover for your holiday? Check that your policy covers you adequately for loss of possessions and valuables, for activities you might want to try – such as scuba-diving, horse-riding, or watersports – and for emergency medical and dental treatment, including flights home if required.

It is worth getting a copy of the E111 form (available from Post Offices) to take with you. This form will ensure that if you have any medical treatment while away you can reclaim the costs incurred on your return. This form must be filled in and stamped before you depart if it is to be valid.

CLIMATE

The weather in the Algarve has attracted tourists to the region for centuries and is one of the most settled in the world. With over three thousand hours of sunshine a year, the climate is similar to that of northern Africa. Winters are generally mild with temperatures rarely dipping below 10°C; summers are hot, often going higher than 30°C. A constant feature of annual climate is the sea breeze, refreshing in the summer, bracing in winter. Rainfall is low and mostly falls in the periods between October and November, and February and March.

It is always worth bringing a light sweater, though for much of the year you will probably be comfortable in shorts and a T-shirt. The hottest period is between June and September and spring temperatures (April-May) are also fairly dependable. Something light to keep out the wind is advisable in all but the hottest months. You will notice in this period that the locals start to wrap up at the slightest easing of the heat. This is simply because they are used to what the Algarve does best: regular high temperatures. Because of this and because the Algarve is a haven for the international holiday maker, the general level of dress is very casual. The only places where you might need something smarter would be in a restaurant in the evening. Some sort of hat is advisable as sea breezes will disguise even the strongest sun.

PETS

Remember to make arrangements for the care of your pets while you are away – book them into a reputable cat or dog hotel, or make arrangements with a trustworthy neighbour to ensure that they are properly fed, watered and exercised while you are on holiday.

SECURITY

Take sensible precautions to prevent your house being burgled while you are away:

- Cancel milk, newspapers and other regular deliveries so that post and milk does not pile up on the doorstep, indicating that you are away.
- Let the postman know where to leave parcels and bulky mail that will not go through your letterbox – ideally with a next-door neighbour.
- If possible, arrange for a friend or neighbour to visit regularly, closing and opening curtains in the evening and morning, and switching lights on and off to give the impression that the house is being lived in.
- Consider buying electrical timing devices that will switch lights and radios on and off, again to give the impression that there is someone in the house.
- Let Neighbourhood Watch representatives and the police know that you will be away so that they can keep an eye on your home.
- If you have a burglar alarm, make sure that it is serviced and working properly and is switched on when you leave (you may find that your insurance policy requires this). Ensure that a neighbour is able to gain access to the alarm to turn it off if it is set off accidentally.
- If you are leaving cars unattended, put them in a garage, if possible, and leave a key with a neighbour in case the alarm goes off.

AIRPORT PARKING AND ACCOMMODATION

If you intend to leave your car in an airport car park while you are away, or stay the night at an airport hotel before or after your flight, you should book well ahead to take advantage of discounts or cheap off-airport parking. Airport accommodation gets booked up several weeks in advance, especially during the height of the holiday season. Check whether the hotel offers free parking for the duration of the holiday – often the savings made on parking costs can significantly reduce the accommodation price.

PACKING TIPS

Baggage allowances vary according to the airline, destination and the class of travel, but 20kg per person is the norm for luggage that is carried in the hold (it usually tells you what the weight limit is on your ticket). You are also allowed one item of cabin baggage weighing no more than 5 kilos, and measuring 46 by 30 by 23cm (18 by 12 by 9 inches). In addition, you can usually carry your duty-free purchases, umbrella, handbag, coat, camera, etc, as hand baggage. Large items – surfboards, golf-clubs, collapsible wheelchairs and pushchairs – are usually charged as extras and it is a good idea to let the airline know in advance that you want to bring these.

CHECK-IN, PASSPORT CONTROL AND CUSTOMS

First-time travellers can often find airport security intimidating, but it is all very easy really.

- Check-in desks usually open two or three hours before the flight is due to depart. Arrive early for the best choice of seats.
- Look for your flight number on the TV monitors in the check-in area, and find the relevant check-in desk. Your tickets will be checked and your luggage taken. Take your boarding card and go to the departure gate. Here your hand luggage will be X-rayed and your passport checked.
- In the departure area, you can shop and relax, but watch the monitors that tell you when to board – usually about 30 minutes before take-off. Go to the departure gate shown on the monitor and follow the instructions given to you by the airline staff.

During your stay

AIRPORTS

The main airport for the Algarve is at Faro, and this is one of the cheapest and most competitive routes in Europe, thanks to the sheer number of charter flights travelling between the UK and the Algarve. Even so, flights are often fully booked during the peak holiday periods, including Christmas: the Algarve is a very popular winter sun destination.

Faro is several miles west of the city and if you land by day from the south you will have a stunning view of the Ria Formosa Nature Reserve, where land and sea meet in a protected zone. The airport has many of the services that you would expect, including a bank, a post office and a tourist office. Several of the vehicle hire companies also have desks. Facilities for eating and shopping have been improved, with new outlets that were opened in the summer of 2001. Faro is the capital of the Algarve region and therefore all transport services are available.

Charter flights can be subject to long delays, so if time is critical, you might be better off paying more to travel by scheduled flight. The Portuguese national carrier, TAP, offers daily flights to the Algarve operating from Heathrow. Some flights are direct, while others involve a change in Lisbon. TAP's UK office is at Gillingham House, 38–44 Gillingham Street, London SW1V 1HU, tel: 0845 601 0932. British Airways also offer charter flights (tel: 0345 222111; www.british-airways.com), as does the no-frills airline, easyJet (www.easyjet.com).

BEACHES

In summer, many beaches have life guards and a flag safety system. Other beaches may be safe for swimming but there are unlikely to be lifeguards or life-saving amenities available. Bear in mind that the strong winds that develop in the hotter months can quickly change a safe beach into a not-so-safe one, and some can have strong currents the further out that you go. If in doubt, ask your local representative or at your hotel.

BEACHES

Flag safety system:
- green = safe bathing and swimming
- yellow = strong swimmers only
- red = no swimming
- chequered = lifeguards not on duty

CHILDREN'S ACTIVITIES

Children are cherished in Portugal and you will find that children are welcome in most restaurants. There is sometimes a separate children's menu available. Most tour operators offer a kids' club in the larger hotels providing appropriate activities for different age groups throughout your stay. This provides them with supervision and friends away from their parents if they choose the activities on offer. A lot of hotels offer a baby-sitting service as well.

In addition to this there are a number of activities in the Algarve available for children. These range from mini-golf to water parks. Places such as equestrian centres and windsurfing clubs often offer lessons for children. These may include organised kids' days with, for example, volleyball, beach games and lunch.

CONSULATE

In most situations your first port of call should be local sources of information or help. If all else fails the British Consulate is at Largo Francisco A. Maurício, Nº7–1º; Portimão; tel. 282 417800.

CURRENCY

Money: In line with the majority of EU member states, Portugal entered the single currency on 1 Jan 2002. Euro (€) note denominations are 500, 200, 100, 50, 20, 10 and 5 €. Coins are 1 and 2 euros and 1, 2, 5, 10, 20 and 50 céntimos.

Banks: are open Mon–Fri 0830–1500. There are exchange shops (*câmbios*) everywhere in the Algarve. You will need to show your passport when exchanging travellers' cheques.

Credit cards: are widely accepted at garages, shops and restaurants in the major towns, but cash is preferred in more rural areas.

CUSTOMS

The Portuguese are a gentle and friendly people. A simple good morning (*Bom dia*) or good afternoon (*Boa tarde*) will delight a perfect stranger. The sense of the family unit is very strong in Portugal; the early evening walkabout and family church are still popular. Unlike the rest of Portugal, the Algarve tends to take a Spanish-style siesta and therefore you may find places closed over lunchtime.

ELECTRICITY

In Portugal they use the standard round-pin European plug. It is a 220-volt system as opposed to the 240-volt UK system.

If you are considering buying electrical appliances to take home, always check that they will work in the UK before you buy.

FACILITIES FOR THE DISABLED

It has been said, in general, that facilities for the disabled are very poor in the Algarve. Many of the ramps and kerbs that have been designed for wheelchairs will make you feel you are mountaineering. Better facilities can be found in the international standard hotels where foreign travel agencies have insisted on them. The situation is slowly improving and most municipal areas will have reasonable facilities. Bus stops have been adapted to enable easier access and there are designated disabled places available on the buses. Many streets are cobbled in Portugal and there are often steep hills or steps. This makes it difficult in general to gain access to a number of places.

GETTING AROUND

Car hire and driving: Portugal has a wide range of vehicle hire companies. All the well-known ones are to be found at the airport. Others can be contacted via your hotel or holiday rep. To hire a car in Portugal you must be over 21 and have held your licence for at least one year. You will need to show your driving licence and carry it with you whenever you are driving. Make sure the insurance cover is sufficient for your needs.

Driving in Portugal can be unpredictable and extreme care needs to be taken. Portuguese drivers can be impatient when faced with a driver who is not used to the area. Many back roads are very narrow and the surfaces may be uneven. However, a lot of main roads have recently been resurfaced and motorways are being extended for easier access to all parts of Portugal.

Rules of the road

- Always carry your driving licence, car hire papers and passport. Police checks are infrequent but you will be fined if you do not have the correct papers.
- Seat belts are compulsory, even for back seat passengers. Children under 12 are not allowed in the front.
- The speed limit is 120kph on motorways, 90kph on highways and 50kph in villages, towns and cities.
- Drink-drive (lower limit than the UK) and speeding laws are rigorously applied.
- The standard of driving is well below that of the UK. Always drive with extreme caution.

Taxis: can be hired from railway stations, bus stations and taxi ranks. If you decide to use a taxi for a longer journey (a day trip for example) it is possible to negotiate the fare. Wherever you go it will help to write down your destination – many drivers speak only limited English.

Buses: operate along the main N125 highway, linking the resorts and main villages. Stops are marked with blue and white *paragem* signs. Timetables are posted at stops. Buses may arrive a little early so leave plenty of time when setting out. Tickets for local buses are sold on board by the driver. Enquire about passes which are sold at bus terminals or from ticket agencies. Express buses operate between the main towns. Tickets must be bought from a bus terminal or ticket agency before boarding. It is advisable to book in advance at the height of the season.

Trains: a railway runs from Vila Real de Santo António near the Spanish border to Lagos in the west and, if you are not in a hurry, this is a good way to see inland Algarve. The trains are clean and airy, if a little basic, and very cheap. Be warned that some stations – Loulé, Silves and Albufeira, for example – are some distance from the town centres.

Mountain bikes, scooters, cycles, mopeds and motorbikes: can all be hired from various outlets in the Algarve. However, due to the poor standard of driving on Portuguese roads, these are not recommended.

HEALTH AND HYGIENE

Health hazards: mosquitoes are attracted by light, so keep your balcony doors or windows closed when the lights are on. Inexpensive anti-mosquito machines which plug into electric sockets are a good investment, as are repellent creams and sprays. To protect yourself against sunburn and its unpleasant effects, never go out without the protection of a high-factor cream. Limit yourself to a few hours sunbathing in the first few days, then gradually increase the amount as your skin adjusts to the climate; also avoid lying out during the hottest hours of the day (1200 to 1500). Always wash the salt off after swimming in the sea and use a moisturising cream to prevent peeling.

Water: tap water in the resorts is safe to drink but has a high mineral content so you may prefer to buy bottled water instead.

MEDIA

There are a few English newspapers published in Portugal. They include the *APN* (Anglo-Portuguese News) and *The News*. They provide stories about national news and events within the English communities. They also give a timetable of cinema showings and theatre events. There is also the *Algarve Gazette* and the *Algarve News*. Many UK newspapers are available in Portugal. You can often buy them on the day of issue, due to the fact that they are printed simultaneously in Spain.

OPENING HOURS

Shops: the majority of shops in Portugal are open from 0900 to 1900 with a break for lunch anywhere between the hours of 1200 and 1500. There are many new shopping centres and these often have longer opening hours, from 1000 to 2300, including Sundays, and no lunch break.

Museums: museums are usually open from 1000 to 1700, again with a break for lunch. Many museums are closed on Mondays as well as public holidays.

Banks: open from 0830 to 1500, Monday to Friday.

Pharmacies: open from 0900 to 1900, with a break for lunch. A sign in the pharmacy window will tell you which pharmacy is open until 2200 and where the all-night pharmacy is.

PERSONAL COMFORT AND SECURITY

For your own personal comfort and security when on holiday it is wise to be cautious. Portugal has a low crime rate, but there are pick- pockets in crowded places as in any other country. Keep your belongings with you all the time or leave them with a friend, for example, if you are going for a dip in the sea. As in other places, women should not travel alone late at night and it is advisable to keep to well-lit areas.

If possible, use a safe in your hotel to keep your valuables in, as this will reassure you and help you to relax and enjoy your holiday without having to worry about security.

If you are taking cash on holiday, only keep a small amount with you in case it gets lost or stolen. Traveller's cheques are always easier to replace.

WHAT TO DO IN AN EMERGENCY

- Dial **112** – the operator will put you through to **police**, **fire brigade**, or **ambulance**.
- Report any theft or accident to the police and your holiday rep, or the hotel staff, who also keep a list of English-speaking doctors and local pharmacies.

24-hour medical assistance

- Albufeira 289 396157
- Loulé 289 410103
- Lagos 282 789811
- Vila Real de Santo António 281 511371

There are First Aid posts at the following beaches: Altura, Alvor, Armação de Pêra, Fuseta, Ilha da Arona, Farol, Manta Rota, Rocha, Sagres and Tavira. Pharmacies will also deal with minor medical problems.

It is possible to get home comforts such as Heinz Baked Beans and English cheddar in the Algarve, as some of the bigger supermarkets cater mainly for English customers. However, holiday makers often like to bring their own tea bags and other home comforts from the UK.

PORTUGUESE

Portuguese people respond warmly to visitors who attempt to speak a little of their language. Here are some words and phrases to help you make a start.

The language

yes	*sim*
no	*não*
thank you	*obrigado (male speaking)/obrigada (female)*
hello	*olá*
goodbye	*adeus*
good morning	*bom dia*
good afternoon	*boa tarde*
good evening/night	*boa noite*
excuse me	*desculpe (I am sorry); com licença (may I pass)*
you're welcome	*de nada*
help!	*socorro!*
how much?	*quanto custa?*

toilets	*sanitários/casa de banho*
gents/ladies	*homens/senhoras*
open	*aberto*
closed	*fechado*
beach	*praia*
church	*igreja*
museum	*museu*
chemist	*farmácia*
do you sell?	*vendem?*
do you speak English?	*fala inglês?*
I don't understand	*não compreendo*
I understand	*compreendo*

Useful words and phrase:
HOTEL

room	*quarto*
single/double	*um quarto simples/quarto duplo*
one/two nights	*uma noite/duas noites*
how much per night?	*quanto custa por noite?*
reservation	*reserva*
toilet	*sanitários/casa de banho*
with bath/shower	*com banho/chuveiro*
Is breakfast included?	*o pequeno almoço está incluído?*

MONEY

bank	*banco*
exchange bureau	*câmbio*
post office	*correio*
postage stamps	*selos*
receipt	*recibo*
credit card	*cartão de credito*
traveller's cheque	*cheque de viagem*

RESTAURANT

restaurant	*restaurante*
table	*mesa*
non-smoking area	*uma área de não fumadores*
menu	*ementa*
tourist menu	*ementa turística*

children's menu	*ementa para crianças*
vegetarian dishes	*pratos vegetarianos*
wine list	*carta de vinhos*
A table for two, please.	*Uma mesa para dois, se faz favor*
smoking/non-smoking	*fumadores/não fumadores*
Another beer, please	*Mais uma cerveja, se faz favor*
Can I see the wine list?	*A carta dos vinhos, se faz favor?*
I'm vegetarian.	*Sou vegetariano.*
Does it contain nuts?	*Contém nozes?*
Can we have the bill, please?	*A conta, se faz favor?*
That's all, thank you.	*Mais nada, obrigado/a*
Where is the bathroom, please?	*Onde e a casa de banho, se faz favor?*

TRAVEL

airport	*aeroporto*
bus	*autocarro*
station	*estação de autocarros*
stop	*paragem*
ticket office	*bilheteira*
a ticket to…	*um bilhete para*
first/second class	*bilhete de primeira classe/segunda classe*
timetable	*horário*
taxi rank	*ponto de táxi*

BY ROAD

petrol	*gasolina*
fill the tank, please	*encha o depósito, por favor*
car park	*parque de estacionamento*
which way to?	*como se vai para?*
left/right	*esquerdo/direito*

POST OFFICE

I'd like to send this to England.	*Queria mandar isto para Inglaterra.*
How much is a stamp for England?	*Quanto custa um selo para mandar para Inglaterra?*
How much is a stamp for a postcard?	*Quanto custa um selo para mandar um postal?*

PHOTOGRAPHY

Can you develop this?	*Podia revelar isto?*
When will it be ready?	*Quando estará pronto?*
a film	*um rolo*
batteries	*as pilhas*

DAYS OF THE WEEK

Monday	*Segunda-feira*
Tuesday	*Terça-feira*
Wednesday	*Quarta-feira*
Thursday	*Quinta-feira*
Friday	*Sexta-feira*
Saturday	*Sábado*
Sunday	*Domingo*
today	*hoje*
tomorrow	*amanhã*
yesterday	*ontem*

NUMBERS

0	*zero*
1	*um/uma*
2	*dois/duas*
3	*trêz*
4	*quatro*
5	*cinco*
6	*seis*
7	*sete*
8	*oito*
9	*nove*
10	*dez*

POST OFFICES

Post offices are known as the *Correios* and they open between 0830 and 1830. There is often a bigger post office in the larger towns, that may open on Saturday mornings as well. Second class post is posted in the red post boxes. First-class post is known as *correio azul* (blue post) and therefore goes in the blue post boxes. You will sometimes see international post boxes as well. There are generally two collections a day – one at 1300 and one at 1800.

RELIGION

Portugal is a predominantly Roman Catholic country and services are held most evenings and every Sunday. There are many saints' days that are celebrated by the Portuguese and these are often public holidays. You may have difficulty sightseeing on these days, since many places will be closed and churches may have extra services. However, if you are lucky enough to be staying in an area when they are having a festival to commemorate one of the saints' days, it is worth joining in with the celebration wherever possible. These are usually joyous events, often with fireworks.

TELEPHONES

Public telephones in Portugal are either coin- or card-operated. Card-operated phones take telephone cards or credit cards. Cards can be purchased in many *tabacarias* (news agents/cigarette shops) and there are also vending machines selling a variety of phone cards in some of the larger post offices.

Many people choose to bring their mobile phones overseas with them. You should check with your mobile phone company before you leave to find out if your mobile will work in Portugal and how much the calls are going to cost you.

PHONING ABROAD

To call an overseas number, dial **00** followed by the country code (UK = **44**). Then the area code (minus the initial 0) and then the number you want.

TIME DIFFERENCES

Portugal is the only other European country on the same time as the UK. Some years ago, Portugal tried to be on the same time as Spain and France, but being so westerly, the daylight versus night time hours just didn't suit them, so they reverted to Greenwich Mean Time.

TIPPING

It is customary, but not essential, to tip in Portugal. If you wish to leave a tip 10 per cent will be gratefully received in restaurants and cafés. You may wish to tip helpful taxi drivers or hotel staff as well.

WEIGHTS AND MEASURES

Weights and measures in Portugal are all metric. Milk, for example is sold in litres rather than pints. In this guide, distances are given in both kilometres (km) and miles.

Shoes sizes and clothes sizes follow the standard European numbering system measured in centimetres. For example, a woman's UK size 5 shoe is equivalent to a 38 European size.

Imperial to metric
1 inch = 2.54 centimetres
1 foot = 30 centimetres
1 mile = 1.6 kilometres
1 ounce = 28 grams
1 pound = 454 grams
1 pint = 0.6 litres
1 gallon = 4.6 litres

Metric to imperial
1 centimetre = 0.4 inches
1 metre = 3 feet, 3 inches
1 kilometre = 0.6 miles
1 gram = 0.04 ounces
1 kilogram = 2.2 pounds
1 litre = 1.8 pints

2003 Edition

For Thomas Cook Publishing:

Publisher: Donald Greig

Project Editor: Charlotte Christensen

Project Administrator: Michelle Warrington

DTP: Steve Collins

Project Management: Cambridge Publishing Management Ltd

Layout and repro: Cambridge Publishing Management Ltd

Index compiled by Indexing Specialists (UK) Ltd

Printed and bound by: Artes Gráficas Elkar, Bilbao, Spain

Acknowledgements

We would like to thank all the photographers, picture libraries and organisations for the loan of the photographs reproduced in this book, to whom copyright in the photograph belongs:

B and E Anderson (page 38);

Pictures Colour Library (page 3);

Thomas Cook Tour Operations Limited (all others).